Managing Public Sport and Leisure Services

ROB

The public sport and leisure sector is both the major provider of sport and leisure facilities and the largest source of employment within the industry. Changes in the government legislation of the industry, as well as growth and development within the sport and leisure industry at large, mean that managers in the public sector have faced a revolution over the last two decades.

This book analyses the issues facing contemporary managers and considers how traditional commercial management techniques can be adapted to present best practice in the management of public services.

Part I: Introduces and contextualises management in the public sport and leisure service.

Part II: Describes and evaluates the key functions of sport and leisure management, including strategic, human resource and financial management, and offers best-practice applications for the public sector.

Part III: Assesses the future of public sector sports and leisure, and analyses the implications for management in the coming years.

Managing Public Sport and Leisure Services allows students to develop an understanding of the complexities and realities of management within the public sector. It provides a unique resource for students following courses in sport and leisure, and public sector management. It also presents an invaluable practical resource for professionals within the industry.

Leigh Robinson is a lecturer in Sport and Leisure Management at the Institute of Sport and Leisure Policy, Loughborough University, UK.

Managing Public Sport and Leisure Services

Leigh Robinson

Routledge
Taylor & Francis Group

LONDON AND NEW YORK

First published 2004 by Routledge
2 Park Square, Milton Park, Abingdon, Oxon, OX14 4RN

Simultaneously published in the USA and Canada
By Routledge
270 Madison Ave, New York NY 10016

Routledge is an imprint of the Taylor & Francis Group

Transferred to Digital Printing 2007

© 2004 Leigh Robinson

Typeset in Sabon by Wearset Ltd, Boldon, Tyne and Wear

British Library Cataloguing in Publication Data
A catalogue record for this book is available from the British Library

Library of Congress Cataloging in Publication Data
A catalog record for this book has been requested

ISBN 0–415–27076–6 (hbk)
ISBN 0–415–27077–4 (pbk)

Printed and bound by CPI Antony Rowe, Eastbourne

For Lisa and Callum

Contents

Illustrations

Figures

Tables

Introduction

The public sector is both the major provider of sport and leisure opportunities and the largest source of employment within this industry. The management of these services has, however, changed fundamentally in recent times. As a result of changes in government legislation, market demands and increasing competition, management of contemporary public sport and leisure services is fundamentally different from that of the 1970s and 1980s. One of the main changes has been the increasing adoption of management approaches and techniques that have been traditionally associated with the commercial sector. Within the past decade, the use of such techniques has become increasingly common in the delivery of public sport and leisure services, as innovative managers have looked to the commercial sector for ideas on how to manage the changing public context.

The adaptations made, and lessons learned, by these managers have been communicated to the industry in a piecemeal and haphazard fashion. Most of the literature available on the use of management techniques in public sport and leisure services is a mixture of rhetoric and/or prescriptive information. In addition, there has been little attempt to systematically consider the application of, or indeed the appropriateness of, public sector use of techniques that are traditionally associated with the commercial sector.

This book aims to fill these gaps and will systematically consider and analyse the issues facing the management of contemporary public sport and leisure services. The book will also evaluate and adapt traditionally commercial management strategies and techniques in order to present best practice in the management of public services. The practical application of the management concepts under review will be highlighted and reported through the use of case study material.

Content and sequencing of the book

Part I The challenge of public sport and leisure management

This section provides an introduction to, and a discussion of, the nature of management in contemporary public sport and leisure services.

CHAPTER 1: THE PUBLIC SPORT AND LEISURE CONTEXT

This chapter sets out the public sport and leisure context, by outlining what this service consists of and how it can be delivered. It also highlights a number of issues that will be discussed in greater detail in later chapters. Finally, it outlines how although sport and leisure management may not be a profession, it is professional in its operations.

CHAPTER 2: THE CHANGING NATURE OF PUBLIC SPORT AND LEISURE MANAGEMENT

The development and management of contemporary public sport and leisure services has been underpinned by three strands of change. First, there has been a growth in consumerism, which has forced managers to respond to increasing customer expectations. Second, changes in legislation affecting public sport and leisure service delivery have impacted upon management, while finally, there has been an increase in the competition facing public sector services. This chapter considers each of these in turn, discussing their impact on the management of these public services and concluding with a detailed analysis of key features in the operating context that directly affect the nature of public sport and leisure management.

CHAPTER 3: MANAGING PUBLIC SPORT AND LEISURE SERVICES

This chapter introduces the principles and functions of managers in the public sport and leisure sector. It considers the skills necessary for effective management, describes possible management styles and ends with analysis and discussion of the implications of culture, power and politics.

Part II The management of public sport and leisure services

The main body of the book consists of six chapters that consider key aspects and functions in the management of public sport and leisure services. Each of the chapters contains:

- an introduction to the management function under consideration;
- a presentation of key issues and best practice in relation to the management function under consideration;
- a discussion of the implications of the public sector context for this function;
- case study material to support the issues under discussion;
- further reading and study questions.

CHAPTER 4: PLANNING AND STRATEGY DEVELOPMENT

This chapter focuses on the concepts of organisational strategy development and planning. It defines strategy and strategic planning, distinguishing between organisational level strategies, service strategies and business plans. The chapter then considers the strategy development and strategic planning process in detail, evaluating how strategy is formulated and implemented within sport and leisure services.

CHAPTER 5: HUMAN RESOURCE MANAGEMENT

In this chapter the issues and procedures involved in the effective management of people are considered. We examine the topics of recruitment, selection, induction, training and development, discipline and conflict. The chapter ends with a consideration of the issues involved in managing 'external workers' such as outreach workers.

CHAPTER 6: FINANCIAL MANAGEMENT

This chapter considers financial management conventions from a public sector perspective. It outlines key terms and addresses aspects of costing, budgeting and financial reporting.

CHAPTER 7: PERFORMANCE MANAGEMENT

This chapter discusses the need for performance management and its role in the delivery of public sport and leisure services. It considers the terminology associated with performance management, evaluates existing performance management systems and focuses, in detail, on performance comparison and performance indicators.

CHAPTER 8: QUALITY MANAGEMENT

This chapter discusses the phenomenon of quality management and its applicability to the public sector. It provides a brief history of the development of the quality movement and considers the appropriateness of the concept within the current public sport and leisure context. The chapter also considers the terminology associated with the quality movement and outlines a variety of frameworks and programmes for the management of quality within public sport and leisure services.

CHAPTER 9: THE MANAGEMENT OF CHANGE

The final chapter of this section explores the multi-faceted nature of change within public sport and leisure organisations. It begins by considering what is meant by organisational change, presenting key approaches to the understanding and management of change. The chapter also considers the barriers to change in public services and ends with a discussion of the methods of successfully introducing changes into public sport and leisure services.

Part III Public sport and leisure management

The final section, consisting of one chapter, revisits the key points that have emerged from the adaptation of best management practice to the public sport and leisure sector.

CHAPTER 10: BEST PRACTICE IN PUBLIC SPORT AND LEISURE
MANAGEMENT

The final chapter of the book offers an overall evaluation of the usefulness of the techniques reviewed. It discusses the key points and trends that emerge from the adaptation of best practice to the public sector and concludes with issues that are likely to impact on the future management of public sport and leisure services.

Part I

The challenge of public sport and leisure management

1 The public sport and leisure context

The structures for delivering sport and leisure within the UK are complex, falling into four broad sectors: local government, education (schools, Further Education and Higher Education establishments), the voluntary sector made up of clubs and national governing bodies and the private sector – the most obvious example of which is the health and fitness industry (DCMS/Strategy Unit, 2002). Of these four sectors, known as the *mixed economy* of sport and leisure, the contribution made by local authorities is substantial and they are recognised as being:

> key providers and enablers of sport and recreation services to local communities, working in partnership with the voluntary and private sectors. They are the biggest providers of sport facilities and provide opportunities through sports development teams and officers who work with the voluntary sector, schools and community.
>
> (DCMS/Strategy Unit, 2002: p. 40)

This chapter aims to establish the nature of the public sport and leisure sector and its management. It provides a brief introduction to the service and then a short overview of the historical development of public provision, highlighting key legislation. It then goes on to discuss the nature of contemporary sport and leisure services.

Public sport and leisure services

Game Plan: A strategy for delivering government's sport and physical activity objectives (DCMS/Strategy Unit, 2002) makes it clear that local authorities are and will continue to be, the major provider of sport, leisure and cultural services. The provision of the majority of facilities outlined in Table 1.1 is discretionary, in that local authorities can choose whether or not they make these available to their community. The exceptions to this are the provision of libraries, playing fields and allotments, whose provision is mandatory.

The rationale for the provision of public sport and leisure services is

Table 1.1 Local authority sport and leisure services

Sport and recreation	Playing fields
	Golf courses
	Bowling greens
	Stadia and tracks
	Marinas
	Ski slopes
	Swimming pools
	Gymnasia
	Sports halls
	Ice rinks
	Leisure centres
Informal recreation	Play spaces
	Open spaces
	Urban parks and gardens
	Beaches, lakes and rivers
Countryside recreation	Country parks
	National parks
	Camping sites
	Picnic sites
	Water sport areas
	Scenic routes and viewing points
Cultural services	Concert halls
	Theatres
	Art galleries
	Art centres
Education-related services	Adult education
	Youth clubs
Library services	Branch libraries
	Mobile libraries
Tourism, conservation and heritage	Information services
	Historic sites
	Nature reserves
	Conservation areas
	Museums
Entertainment, catering and conferences	Public halls
	Pavilions
	Piers
	Restaurants
	Bars
	Conference centres
Housing, community and social services	Play centres
	City farms
	Allotments
	Day centres
	Community centres
	Holiday camps
	Caravan parks

Source: Adapted from Torkildsen, 1999.

based on two main arguments. First, there is the market failure argument. Local authorities provide sport and leisure services for those who cannot afford the opportunities offered by the other sectors. Gratton and Taylor (2000) provide a comprehensive overview of the efficiency- and equity-related reasons for public provision and it is apparent from their discussions and the analyses of Coalter (1998) and Stabler and Ravenscroft (1994) that a key motivation for state provision is to ensure access for all citizens to sport and leisure opportunities through price subsidies and targeted programming.

Second, there are also several arguments about the 'externalities' of sport and leisure participation (Gratton and Taylor, 2000; Nichols and Taylor, 1993), which suggest that participation is beneficial to society. Participation in sport and leisure, in addition to being intrinsically valuable, has also been identified as having extrinsic benefits such as the potential to improve health, reduce crime, improve educational standards and contribute towards lifelong learning (DCMS, 1999). Thus, public sport and leisure services are expected to deliver objectives relating to access, the rights of citizenship to sport and leisure and the external benefits to society of participation. These social objectives have traditionally provided the justification for the provision and subsidy of public sport and leisure services.

The provision of sport and leisure opportunities by the public sector has been a relatively recent phenomenon as, although historically providing for a limited range of opportunities such as parks and libraries, it was the 1970s before the wider public sector role in sport and leisure provision was firmly established. This occurred primarily through the provision of multi-purpose facilities, which emerged as a result of a massive investment in leisure brought about by the 1974 re-organisation of local government. The extent of this investment was significant in that there was a ten-fold increase in the number of sports centres and a 50 per cent increase in the number of swimming pools between 1972 and 1978 (Henry, 2001). As a result, by the end of the 1970s, the sport and leisure facility framework that exists today was practically in place.

Local authorities do not, however, only provide facilities. As outlined above, they have two other key roles in the provision of sport and leisure. First, local authorities have an 'enabling' role in that they enable community groups and schools to provide opportunities by providing access to facilities, equipment and financial assistance. The second, and perhaps more important role, is in the widening of participation in sport and leisure, which is carried out primarily by sports development and community workers who deliver services within communities, rather than at a single central specialised location. The combination of these three roles means that the public sector is the major provider of UK sport and leisure opportunities.

The nature and management of the public sport and leisure sector has changed markedly since the late 1980s. Government legislation, increasing consumer expectations, increasing competition and the increasing professionalism of those who manage public services has resulted in a public sector that delivers services via local authority staff, through the establishment of charitable trusts or in partnership with the commercial sector. This hybrid of delivery arrangements will be discussed later in the chapter: however, as a result of these options it is not always immediately obvious what sport and leisure opportunities can be considered part of the public sector and what are part of the charitable and commercial sectors.

Nonetheless, there are several factors that categorise services as being public sector services, no matter who is responsible for their delivery. These factors are:

- local authority staff deliver the service;
- the local authority owns the facility or provides a substantial part of the funding for the building of the facility;
- the local authority provides a substantial part of the funding for the running of the service;
- the local authority maintains control of the objectives of the service via contractual arrangements;
- the service is required to meet social objectives;
- managers of the service are either directly or indirectly accountable to local politicians.

There are a number of characteristics, which are discussed in Chapter 2, that arise as a result of being a public service. These affect the delivery of sport and leisure, no matter who is responsible for the service management. Thus, this book focuses on the management of public sport and leisure services, rather than on managing in the public sector. This is because many of those who manage public services will come from either the commercial or charitable sectors. It is recognised that the sector background of those who manage the service is less important than the fact that the service is the ultimate responsibility of the public sector.

In addition, sport and leisure services are different from many other local authority services and these differences make their management increasingly complex. First, as outlined earlier, the provision of most of these services is discretionary, making the service susceptible to budget cuts, low prioritisation and outsourcing (Nichols and Robinson, 2000). Second, sport and leisure services have the capacity to generate income for the local authority. The ability to generate revenue by charging fees, attracting expenditure on food and drink and through the provision of venues for major events actually protects these services against the problems outlined above. This does, however, put pressure on managers to maximise revenue, which conflicts with the social objectives outlined earlier. The need to deliver both operational and social objectives is the third factor that makes sport and leisure different from other local authority services. Few services are required to deliver subsidised services to parts of the community who cannot afford other sport and leisure opportunities and generate revenue from those who can. Fourth, and associated with a previous point, sport and leisure services compete with the commercial and voluntary sectors for customers. This means that many public sport and leisure services need to be managed as though they were businesses, to generate the revenue that protects them from budget cuts that may occur as a result of their discretionary nature. These points make the management of sport and leisure services fundamentally different from the management of other local authority services.

The development of public sport and leisure services

The historical development of public sport and leisure services has been extensively discussed by Coalter (1990) and Henry (2001) and therefore the following section only provides a brief overview of the key developments in public sector provision. Public sport and leisure provision can be considered to have gone through three distinct phases, which have led to the framework of provision that is apparent today. The first of these phases occurred prior to the start of the twentieth century and laid the foundations for local authority provision of sport and leisure. The second and somewhat lengthy phase occupied most of the twentieth century and established local authorities as key providers of sport and leisure opportunities. The third phase, in which local authorities currently operate, commenced in the late 1980s and has challenged the role of local authorities in providing sport and leisure services. Table 1.2 outlines key legislation that affects the provision of these services.

Prior to the 1980s, central government involvement in public sport and leisure provision had been experienced spasmodically. Unlike other publicly provided services such as housing and waste management, central government had never taken on a role as a direct provider of sport and leisure services and the nineteenth century Acts affecting service provision were, and have remained, enabling rather than mandatory. This historical reluctance to become directly involved in sport and leisure provision reinforced the need for the already present, non-governmental providers, which led to the mixed economy of leisure that is apparent today (Coalter, 1990; Henry, 2001). The prominent roles of the commercial and voluntary sectors, established in the nineteenth century and continued ever since, have allowed central government to argue that there was no need for direct intervention. This differentiated sport and leisure from many other local authority services, particularly during the creation of the Welfare State, where, in contrast to the provision of universal services, central government concern with sport and leisure was focused on the provision of excellence, with the establishment of the Arts Council in 1946 and the

Table 1.2 Key legislation in the provision of public sport and leisure services

Act	Purpose
Baths and Wash-Houses Act (1846)	Concerned with personal cleansing and hygiene, but led to the provision of swimming pools
Public Health Act (1875)	Enabled urban authorities to purchase, lease, lay out, plant, improve and maintain land for public walks or pleasure grounds
Public Health Act (1936)	Authority to provide public baths and wash-houses, swimming baths and bathing places and the authority to close them to the public for use by schools or clubs and to charge admission
Physical Training and Recreation Act (1937)	Encouraged a movement towards national fitness. Local authorities could acquire land for facilities and clubs
Town and Country Planning Acts (1947, 1971, 1974)	Made it possible for local authorities to define the sites of proposed public buildings, pleasure grounds, open spaces and nature reserves
National Parks and Access to the Countryside Act (1949). The Countryside Act (1968)	Local planning authorities who had responsibility for national parks were allowed to provide accommodation and camping grounds and make provision for recreation
Education Acts (1918, 1944)	Allowed and then made it mandatory for schools to provide adequate facilities for recreation, social and physical training
Public Libraries and Museums Act (1964)	Made it statutory for every authority to provide a comprehensive and efficient library service
Local Government (miscellaneous provisions) Act (1976)	Permitted local authorities to provide such recreational activities as they think fit
Local Government Act (1988)	Introduced compulsory competitive tendering into the management of sport and leisure facilities
Local Government Act (1999)	Introduced the duty of Best Value into the management of public sport and leisure services

development of the National Centres of Excellence during the post-war period.

It was the 1960s before central government began to consider sport and leisure as a relatively distinct policy area. This change in attitude was brought about by the findings of the 1957 Wolfenden Committee on Sport which recommended the development of policy relating to sport and leisure aimed at social control and improving the health of the nation (Henry,

2001; Houlihan, 1991). In addition, there was a perceived need to enhance Britain's prestige at international competition. What was arguably more important, however, was the increasing demand from the general public for wider access to sport and recreation opportunities and as a consequence, although still refraining from making provision mandatory, central government policy began to address the public provision of sport and leisure.

This led to the appointment of a Minister for Sport in 1962, the establishment of the Advisory Sports Council in 1965 and the adoption of a policy of 'Sport for All' in 1966. It was the latter which had the most direct impact on local authorities as the commitment to 'Sport for All' led to a rapid increase in the number of facilities provided by the public sector as attempts were made to provide opportunities for expressed demand. As a consequence, the role of local authorities in sport and leisure provision, predominantly as providers of facilities, became firmly established in the eyes of the community.

Central government involvement was then evident in the 1970s in a range of 'Recreation as Welfare' policies that deployed targeted forms of sport and leisure provision as strategies to alleviate problems among the more deprived population sectors and areas of the country (Henry, 2001). For the most part, however, direct provision of these services lay in the hands of local government, with local authority expenditure rising unevenly but persistently from the mid-1970s onward.

At this time however, the Welfare State and its management were facing rising criticisms over alleged inefficiency and ineffectiveness (Elcock, 1996). The Welfare State encouraged greater public spending in order to support welfare programmes and placed excessive tax burdens on the public. Criticisms aimed at the management of public services were made by political commentators and the public at large, focusing on the absence of financial management systems and the lack of measures of performance and cost control. In addition, it was argued that the professionals responsible for the running of public services lacked appropriate managerial skills and by 1978 public disillusion with local authority services was at its greatest (Elcock, 1996).

Radical change to the management of these services began with the election of the Conservative Government in 1979. Elcock (1996: p. 180) described this government as being 'innately hostile' to local authorities, seeing them as 'bloated, unresponsive bureaucracies which needed to be converted into leaner, fitter organisations'. This hostility was still evident in the report *Performance Review in Local Government* released by the Audit Commission (1988: p. 1), nearly a decade later. Here it was stated that the continued existence of local government 'depends on its ability to be competitive, offer consumer choice and provide well managed, quality services'. The underlying belief of central government was that the way the commercial sector was managed should be the model followed in the public sector.

Many local authorities were, however, slow to adopt the management techniques advocated by the Conservative Government. In response, the government developed a series of policy initiatives that were intended to force local authorities to operate in a manner that reflected the commercial sector. The most prominent of these initiatives was a radical and deeply unpopular piece of legislation called Compulsory Competitive Tendering (CCT). Introduced via the Planning and Land Act (1980) and the Local Government Act (1988), CCT was designed to ensure that the provision of many local authority services was opened up to market competition. This meant that local authorities no longer had the automatic right to provide the services they had traditionally been responsible for. They could only do this if they won the right to do so against competition.

Compulsory Competitive Tendering

Although libraries, museums and galleries remained exempt from Compulsory Competitive Tendering, the legislation was introduced into other sport and leisure services in 1989, with two main objectives (Audit Commission, 1989; Audit Commission, 1993). First, it was expected to decrease the costs of public sport and leisure services by ensuring that the service was run in the most efficient manner possible. This efficiency was judged solely on the bottom-line cost of the service provision. Second, it aimed to improve services to users, by encouraging service providers to improve service quality to attract customers. In order to do this, CCT was required to be applied to the management of the following facilities:

- swimming pools, skating rinks, gymnasia;
- tennis courts, squash courts, badminton courts, pitches for team games, athletics grounds;
- tracks and centres for bicycles, golf courses, putting greens, bowling greens, bowling centres, bowling alleys;
- riding centres, courses for horse racing, artificial ski slopes, centres for flying, ballooning or parachuting and centres for boating or water sports on inland or coastal waters.

The only facilities exempt from CCT were those provided from premises not predominantly used for sport or physical recreation, such as social clubs or those on premises occupied by educational institutions, such as schools. From the above list, it is apparent that CCT affected the management of nearly all sport and leisure services, in particular those that were able to generate income.

CCT had substantial implications for the organisation of sport and leisure departments. Providers were required to keep accounts for individual contracts, rather than managing one large budget as they had done in the past. In addition, they were required not to act in an 'anticompetitive' manner, which meant that they had to ensure that all potential bidders, both those from within the organisation and those without, had access to exactly the same information and documentation. Most importantly, CCT led to the restructuring of departments into Client and Contractor sections. The Client section awarded and oversaw the contract, while the Contractor section, known as the Direct Service Organisation (DSO), tendered a bid to run the contract and in 82 per cent of local authorities won the right to manage the facilities.

The CCT process was relatively straightforward. Local authorities were required to advertise that their sport and leisure management contracts were open to tender and to encourage interested parties to express their interest. These parties were then assessed by the local authority in terms of their ability to run the contract and from this a short list of competent contractors was compiled. Those on the short list were then invited to offer – or tender – a bid for managing the services. Once all the sealed bids had been received, the local authority determined the best bid, usually on the basis of price and agreed service levels and then awarded the contract.

Contracts were usually awarded for a period of five to ten years and were awarded to one of three main types of management (Henry, 2001). First, as highlighted above, the majority of contracts were awarded to existing local authority staff, the Direct Service Organisation. Set up as a separate section of the service, the DSO was responsible for the management of the facilities covered by the contract and reported to the Client section. Contracts were also awarded to 'management buyouts', where the local authority workforce had set itself up as a private company to tender for and run the facilities. Finally, contracts were awarded to external contractors, usually from the commercial sector, who then became responsible for the delivery of these public services.

Replaced in 1999 by Best Value, the impact of CCT on the management of public sport and leisure services was significant. This is discussed in detail in Chapter 2; however, it is worth noting that CCT was a major factor in bringing about change in the style of management to be found in these services.

Best Value

Although acknowledging the role of CCT in improving cost management and widening service provision, the Labour Party strongly criticised the CCT legislation for promoting a universal focus on costs to the exclusion of social objectives and quality. In order to address this, the Local Government Act of 1999 made the delivery of 'Best Value' services mandatory.

Based on the principles of accountability, transparency, continuous improvement and ownership, the underlying rationale for Best Value is a concern with quality, effectiveness, performance measurement and customer focus. A central commitment to commercial management is inherent in Best Value which is seen as being 'not just about economy and efficiency, but also about effectiveness and the quality of local services' (Armstrong, 1997: p. 2).

The performance management framework of Best Value is discussed in detail in Chapter 4; however, it is based on a structure known as the four Cs, which local authorities are required to follow in their implementation of this legislation. They are expected to:

> *Challenge* the rationale for the continued provision of services and the manner in which they are provided. Local authorities need to ask themselves why they are delivering the service or services under review. Often the provision of public services has more to do with custom and habit than need, and the local authority must not only challenge the way the service is being delivered, but ask if the service is needed at all. If this challenge is done properly, at the end of the review the local authority should be clear about why it provides a service in the manner that it does, or it will have identified alternative methods of provision.

> *Consult* with all relevant stakeholders at important stages of the review process. The legislation contains a statutory requirement to carry out consultation when completing the Best Value process. Local authorities are required to consult with stakeholders, who are the people with a vested interest in the service, including taxpayers, service users and local businesses.

> *Compare* performance with others, both nationally and locally and against local performance indicators derived in consultation with stakeholders. This allows local authorities to identify how they are performing against other authorities and against the targets felt to be important by the local community.

> Demonstrate *competitiveness* of service delivery through a rigorous comparison with alternative services and providers. The duty of Best Value means that services should not be delivered directly by local authorities if a more efficient and effective provider exists.
>
> (DETR, 1998a)

The information gathered via this structure needs to be incorporated into the performance framework highlighted in Chapter 2 and discussed in detail in Chapter 4. The Audit Commission then audits performance against the strategies produced by this process.

Best Value has addressed many of the weaknesses of CCT. However, concerns over the fragmented approach taken to Best Value by some local authorities has led central government to introduce a new programme of legislation – Comprehensive Performance Assessment (CPA).

Comprehensive Performance Assessment

The Comprehensive Performance Assessment framework, launched in 2002, aims to build upon Best Value (Office of the Deputy Prime Minister, 2002). Still based on the four Cs approach, CPA extends the principles of Best Value by incorporating the following principles:

- clearly defined priorities and exacting performance standards developed with local government;
- regular comprehensive performance assessments for all councils, identifying how they are performing against standards;
- co-ordinated incentives, rewards and tools which address the results of the comprehensive assessments and drive service improvement, including:
  - clear and concise public information about councils' performance;
  - integrated inspection programmes tailored to councils' strengths, weaknesses and needs;
  - additional freedoms, powers and flexibility over resources for councils with the track record and capacity to use them;
  - tough action to tackle failing councils and services;
  - stretching targets and rewards for service improvement, through local public service agreements;
  - a streamlined, proportionate and integrated Best Value regime.
  (Office of the Deputy Prime Minister, 2002).

Although it is not clear how CPA will be applied to public services, the principles of objective-led performance management and review are still a fundamental part of the new legislation. There appear to be three main differences between Comprehensive Performance Assessment and Best Value. First, local authorities will have to demonstrate how their services work together to contribute to the government's priorities of education, health, crime and transport. This implies less emphasis on individual service reviews and more focus on the integration of services to contribute to overall strategic issues.

Second, it appears that audits will be made of local authorities as a whole, rather than at the service level, as happens with Best Value. This will reinforce the need for a planning process that is based on the determination of strategic objectives, with integrated plans and performance management frameworks. Third, and in recognition of the effectiveness of some local authorities, through the process of CPA central government intends on loosening controls on financing for those authorities who are delivering good services. Thus, the planning process becomes increasingly important under CPA, to assist councils to achieve their objectives and consequently gain more control over their services.

Public sport and leisure delivery mechanisms

One of the most significant impacts that Best Value has had on public sport and leisure has been to encourage local authorities to investigate alternative ways of delivering these services. One of the fundamental questions required of local authorities under the Best Value and CPA frameworks is whether local authorities should continue to provide the services they do or whether an alternative provider would be more effective. Research carried out by the Audit Commission (2002, p. 16) showed that the four main options explored by those providing sport and recreation services are:

- continuation of in-house provision: the local authority continues to provide the service as they had done prior to Best Value. For many local authorities, the services will be managed and delivered by the Direct Service Organisation that was successful in winning the CCT contract;
- externalisation or partnership with a private sector provider: occurs when the local authority contracts out the management of their sport and leisure service to a commercial company;
- setting up a trust: an increasing number of authorities are transferring their facilities into an industrial provident society or a company limited by guarantee with charitable status. Both operate as non-profit distributing organisations, which have become known as 'trusts'. This transfer is primarily due to the financial savings that can be gained by the rate and tax relief that trusts can claim (Collins, 2003). Usually, the trust leases the building from the local authority for an extended period and is then responsible for delivering the service. The managers of trusts answer to a panel of trustees, who oversee operations for a set period of time. In most cases the management of the service continues to be carried out by the staff who were responsible for the facility when it was part of the local authority;
- a public/private partnership: this is a new and somewhat complex arrangement when, in exchange for a lengthy management contract, the commercial company invests in the facilities that provide the service. There are two main benefits of this. First, partnerships provide funding that local authorities could not, or would not afford. Second, the private sector assumes some of the financial risk that the public sector would otherwise carry.

In reality, many local authorities are using a combination of these methods in order to deliver sport and leisure services. For example, Sheffield City Council delivers its sport and recreation services through a combination of in-house provision, partnership with the private sector and charitable trusts, as outlined in Figure 1.1.

Sheffield City Trust facilities

Ponds Forge International Sports Centre

Concord Leisure Centre

Sheffield City Hall

Woodbourne Road Athletics Track

Beauchief Golf Course

Tinsley Golf Course

Hillsborough Leisure Centre

Sheffield Arena

Don Valley Stadium

iceSheffield

Birley Golf Course

The Trust also leases the Enfield Pub opposite the Arena

All of these facilities (with the exception of iceSheffield) have Sheffield City Council as the ultimate head landlord, with leases existing until at least 2024. Facility management is delivered by Sheffield International Venues, the operating arm of the City Trust. The exception is the Hallam FM Arena, which is on management contract to Clear Channel Entertainment.

Beauchief and Birley Golf Courses are operated by the Trust under lease and have established clubs based at both. Tinsley Golf Course is operated at present by Sheffield International Venues on a management contract to the Council. This is because of Charity Commission issues relating to the clubhouse and golf course partly intruding on parkland held as a charitable trust by the Council.

Council-operated facilities

Stocksbridge Sports Centre

Heeley Pool

Graves Tennis and Leisure Centre

These are operated directly by the council and managed by the head of the former in-house DSO. The transfer of Graves to a private sector operator has been agreed and discussions with a preferred operator are well advanced, but the transfer is not likely to take place until 2004. Planning permission has been granted for the redevelopment of the joint public/private facility they intend to operate.

The long-term plan is to outsource Stocksbridge and Heeley also, possibly to some kind of community trust.

Sport and Community Recreation Section

The Client element of Sport and Community Recreation within Leisure Services continues to manage Verdon Recreation Centre, two adventure playgrounds and the Underbank Outdoor Activity Centre at Midhopestones.

Private-sector-operated facilities

Concord Golf Course is out on a 25-year lease to a local golf professional who has added a driving range and offers Pay and Play Golf, plus a Club operation. It is also intended to place Graves Tennis and Leisure Centre out into the private sector, as referred to above.

Community-managed facilities (trusts)

Upperthorpe Pool: transferred on a lease to the Upperthorpe Health Living Centre Trust.

Chapeltown Pool: building owned by Ecclesfield Parish Council, building licensed to Chapeltown Pool Group, a community business who operate it with funding from City Council and the Parish Council.

King Edwards Pool: transferred to a trust operation with no direct funding from the Council. The facility now makes an operating surplus, primarily through the provision of swimming lessons.

Dual-use sports facilities on school sites

Westfield Sports Centre

Springs Leisure Centre

Waltheof Sports Centre

These are directly managed by the schools and receive a grant from Sport and Community Recreation.

Facilities built using PPP at secondary school sites

Firvale School

King Edwards

Tapton

Ecclesfield

All comprise a sports hall, activity room and artificial turf pitch. They are operated by Interserve who generate income from lettings outside school time.

Figure 1.1 Management of sport and leisure facilities in Sheffield.

Public sport and leisure service personnel

The legislation described above provides the framework within which sport and leisure services must be delivered. The actual delivery of these services is the responsibility of three types of personnel: politicians, sport and leisure officers and service managers and staff. Table 1.3 provides examples of the roles that can be held by public sport and leisure personnel.

Local authority politicians, also known as councillors or members, are considered to be ultimately responsible for the services delivered and the standards at which they are delivered. In theory, they decide policy, what is to be built and where and they have final control over budgets (Torkildsen, 1999). An elected member should use the resources of the authority to establish sport and leisure needs and wants, establish priorities, make decisions and then pass this information on to service staff to implement. They should then monitor the progress of their decisions and evaluate performance against performance measures. In practice, however, although members hold the authority and power to make strategic decisions, they are heavily reliant on advice given to them by sport and leisure officers (Nichols, 1996; Robinson, 1999a).

This is because sport and leisure officers are the staff actually responsible for generating the policy that is discussed and agreed by elected members. Torkildsen (1999) suggested that officers must inform, educate and influence elected members and in most authorities, it is the officers who establish objectives and priorities and develop strategic plans, which they then monitor. They report on progress to elected members, who are reliant on their expertise and skill. The final category of staff comprises those responsible for actually delivering the sport and leisure service, ranging from managers of facilities, to leisure assistants and outreach workers. The last two groups of personnel are the professionals responsible for delivering public sport and leisure services.

The professionalisation of public sport and leisure management

Being viewed as a profession is the goal of many occupational groups, as professional status conveys a perception of expertise, specialist knowledge and skills and control over work and over those entering the industry (Houlihan, 2001). Sport and leisure management is no different from other occupations and those employed within the industry have, over a period of time, sought to achieve professional status. The process by which occupations move towards professional status is known as professionalisation and is typically indicated by these features:

- the practice of the occupation is founded on the basis of sound theoretical knowledge whose application is valued in society;

Table 1.3 Positions in sport and leisure services

Officers	Client officer
	Performance manager
	Policy manager
	Quality officer
	Projects officer
	Disability officer
	Sports development manager
	Team leader for play, countryside, tourism, arts, museums
	Best Value officer
	Marketing manager
	Leisure card manager
Service deliverers	Facility manager
	Leisure assistant
	Lifeguard
	Fitness assistant
	Sports development worker
	Gallery assistant
	Museum curator
	Events manager
	Sponsorship assistant
	'Learn to swim' teacher
	Sports coach
	Receptionist
	Cleaner

- the acquisition of this knowledge is founded on a long period of education and training;
- the occupation subscribes to an ideal of altruistic public service rather than being motivated solely by profit;
- the occupational group has control over recruitment and can regulate entry;
- there is a well-organised colleague group which uses disciplinary powers to enforce an ethical code of conduct.

(Coalter, 1990: p. 173)

Although initially emerging within the late 1960s, the concept of sport and leisure management as a potential profession gained momentum in the 1970s in response to the rapid expansion in the number of facilities that emerged as a result of local government reorganisation in 1974 (Houlihan, 2001; Torkildsen, 1999). The need to improve the quality of the management of the sport and leisure industry was highlighted in the 1975 White Paper *Sport and Recreation*, and then took increasing prominence with the establishment of the Yates Committee in 1977. This committee had the remit of reviewing the state of sport and leisure management and making recommendations on the training of staff (Houlihan, 2001).

During this period a number of features suggested that sport and leisure management was moving towards professional status. First, Henry (2001) described how the Institute of Leisure and Amenity Management (ILAM) was established in 1979. In the early 1980s, this unified professional body:

> established a curriculum for professional training and sought to use the associated membership examinations as a means of controlling access to both the Institute itself and to junior, middle and senior management posts in leisure.
>
> (Henry, 2001: p. 149)

Second, in 1969 the first postgraduate qualification in Recreation Management became available at Loughborough University. Although a number of professional bodies and institutes, such as the Institute of Sport and Recreation Management (ISRM) and the Recreation Managers' Association, had been providing technical training and qualifications for some time, this was the first course to focus on the *management* of the industry. Since then there has been a remarkable increase in the number of educational institutions offering sport and leisure management programmes (Hanson, Minten and Taylor, 1998), with over 1,000 courses being offered that contain the words sport and/or leisure in the title. The consequence of these courses is better qualified staff, at all levels of the industry.

These two features appear to indicate the evolution of sport and leisure management as a profession. However, in the mid-1980s, Murphy (1986) used the characteristics of a profession, as outlined above, to assess the status of sport and leisure management and concluded that it was not a profession. This was supported by Coalter *et al.* (1986: p. 88) who also argued that the establishment of a profession was not desired by so-called leisure professionals, as their desire for the benefits of professional status was 'tempered by a concern that the process of professionalisation, of qualification and enhanced status could become an end in itself'. Both Murphy (1986) and Coalter *et al.* (1986) had concerns about the accessibility of leisure, suggesting that the ease with which people could make their own decisions about leisure would make it difficult for professionals to derive status from expertise and judgement. This point was picked up at a later stage by Houlihan (2001) in his discussion of how CCT had weakened the move towards professional status. He also noted that:

> part of the difficulty that sport and recreation service managers faced in furthering their professional aspirations was that even on the client side senior managers were operating within an environment that was not conducive to the exercise of judgement or the development of organisational autonomy.
>
> (Houlihan, 2001: p. 5)

Houlihan (2001) went on to add that by the mid-1990s the professional bodies had still not been particularly successful at controlling entry to the

Table 1.4 Changing management styles in public sport and leisure services

Timescale	Early 1970s	Late 1970s/early 1980s	Mid-1980s	Late 1980s/early 1990s	Late 1990s
Management focus	Facility focus	Activity/group focus	Community focus	Market focus	Quality focus
Objectives	Maximise income	Maximise participation	Maximise opportunities for 'problem groups'	Economic revenue and economic efficiency	Maximise quality and achieve best value
Management styles	Centralised	Decentralised	Decentralised, advocacy, catalytic role	Expert marketeer	Agent of organisational change
Mode of consultation	Professional	Consultant	Partnership	Market research	Customer surveys
Attitudes to client	Regulation/control of users	Encouragement of under-users	Positive support of disadvantaged	Identify appropriate market segments; customer care	Citizens: one among groups of stakeholders
Programme emphases	Reactive	Informal, fun and sociability, elitism played down	Proactive, creative, developmental	Selling lifestyle, health and fitness	Meeting corporate goals through leisure
Government initiatives	Local government reorganisation	White Paper: Sport and Recreation	Urban programmes; Sports Council	CCT	Best Value

Source: Adapted from Henry, 2001.

field, nor at ensuring that those wishing to be employed in the field obtained specific qualifications. It was apparent that the myriad of graduate/postgraduate and professional courses that had become available actually worked against the strategies of ILAM and ISRM. Thus, it would appear that sport and leisure management has not evolved to become a profession.

However, whether or not it is a profession, there is no doubt that public sport and leisure managers have become increasingly competent, innovative and skilled in the way that they manage their services. In short, the management of these services has become increasingly professional in its approach to delivery. Employees are becoming increasingly qualified in management at both undergraduate and postgraduate level, which inevitably leads to an industry in which staff at all levels are appropriately trained, not just in technical skills, but also in the skills necessary to manage the service effectively.

Henry (2001) has identified how the style of public sport and leisure management has changed (Table 1.4) as it has adapted to external influences. Perhaps most importantly, evidence offered by Robinson (1999a) shows that public professionals were responsible for making decisions regarding the implementation of management practices. These decisions were then communicated to local councillors who, on the whole, accepted the decision with little debate (Nichols, 1996; Robinson 1999a). The acceptance by politicians of this directive approach is a key indicator of the perceived professionalism of public sport and leisure personnel.

Summary and Conclusions

This chapter has provided an overview of the factors that have influenced the development of contemporary public sport and leisure services. The following chapter goes on to consider the impact of these factors in more detail, in particular outlining their effect on management.

2 The changing nature of public sport and leisure management

The way public sport and leisure services are managed has changed markedly over the past two decades as a result of the increasingly professional practices of those who are managers in the industry. This change has resulted in the emergence of a style of management called *new managerialism*, which is characterised by the use of management techniques that have usually only been found in the commercial sector. This chapter discusses the emergence of this style of management and identifies the features of new managerialism. It then highlights the factors that have led to the development of new managerialism within public services. It concludes by discussing the features of the public sector context that make the management of these services different from that of the commercial and voluntary sectors.

Introduction

Public services have traditionally been seen as bureaucratic organisations managed in a style that places importance on committees, procedures and administration. The public sector has historically been considered slow to change, thought to be internally focused and reactive in comparison with the market-orientated, proactive commercial sector. For a variety of reasons, to be discussed below, public services, and in particular sport and leisure services, are no longer managed in such a manner. Techniques such as strategic planning, quality management and performance management are now commonplace within the management of these services.

The use of such techniques has resulted in a style of management that is called new public management or new managerialism (Robinson, 1999a). An exact definition of new managerialism is difficult to find: however, this management style is based on the 'assumption that better management will prove an efficient (solution) for a wide range of economic and social ills' (Pollitt, 1993: p. 1).

Examples of the techniques of new managerialism within public services are, however, relatively easy to find and Horton and Farnham (1999) highlighted the following features as evidence of new managerialism within UK public services:

- an approach to management which is driven by objectives, plans, budgets, performance indicators and quality standards;
- benchmarking carried out against commercial business standards to evaluate performance;
- managers who are prepared to facilitate change, rather than resisting it;
- individual performance reviews that ensure that staff focus on agreed objectives;
- a concern with the customer rather than the service.

From a public sport and leisure perspective, the characteristics of new managerialism outlined above are inherent within the management of these services and a detailed discussion of these techniques follows in the second part of the book. For example, as outlined in Chapter 4, planning and strategy development is required for all public sport and leisure services and, as a result, managers produce local cultural strategies and service plans to meet the objectives of these strategies. Chapter 7 outlines the process of performance management that has been adopted, which utilises performance targets and indicators. Finally, Chapter 8 discusses the widespread use of quality management techniques used by managers in order to deliver services of a high quality.

New managerialism has had many benefits. Services are now 'leaner and meaner' with less staff, less waste and increased productivity (Horton and Farnham, 1999). Managers have adopted a more rational approach to decision making and the allocation of resources (Nichols, 1996). Strategic planning is now commonplace, as is quality management and performance monitoring (Robinson, 1999a). Most importantly, managers have become more responsive to those using their service. Overall, public managers have become more concerned with the efficiency and effectiveness of their services.

At this point it is useful to define what is meant by efficiency and effectiveness as these are terms that are used frequently throughout the book. Efficiency is concerned with the amount of output that is achieved for a given resource input. For example, a measure of efficiency would be the number of children in a swimming class in relation to the number of staff involved. If a class has two members of staff and 20 children, it is more efficient than a class with three members of staff and 20 children.

Effectiveness is the quality of the outcome in relation to the resources used. For instance, it could be the number of children that actually learned to swim 50 metres by attending the classes. If the three members of staff teach all of their children to swim 50 metres, they are more effective than the two members of staff who only teach nine children to swim this far. This is because each of the three staff taught five children to swim the distance, while in the class with only two staff, one taught five children to swim 50 metres, but the other only taught four.

The emergence of new managerialism

Research carried out by Robinson (1999b) found that new managerialism had emerged within public sport and leisure services as a result of the actions and interactions of a variety of factors in the public sector environment (Figure 2.1). The senior managers interviewed in her research felt that the biggest change required of them, in recent times, was the need to be competitive within the leisure market. This transformation was initiated by increasing pressure from consumers and market competition which, facilitated by the increasing professionalism of those working in the industry, as outlined in the previous chapter, led to the emergence of new managerialism. Central government legislation was thought to have accelerated the process as it required greater competitiveness and thus increased the use of new managerialism techniques.

Consumerism and the development of the customer focus in local authorities

The consumer movement, which began in the 1950s, has had a significant impact on organisations that provide goods and services. Brought about by customers joining together to increase their power, Pfeffer and Coote (1991) outlined how the consumer movement led to a legal right to protection from poor quality goods and services and improvements in service quality. Represented by the Consumers' Association in the UK, the consumer movement facilitated a number of initiatives that protected

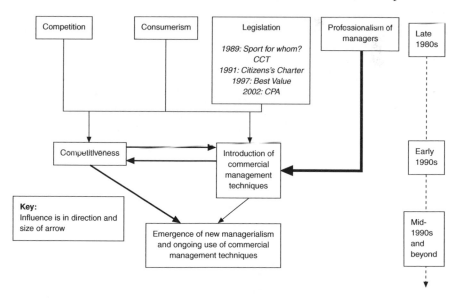

Figure 2.1 Factors leading to the development of new managerialism in public sport and leisure services.

customers from poor-quality goods and services. First, the consumer movement brought about a requirement for businesses to provide information on the cost, quality and components of their goods and services so that customers could make more informed choices. Second, the Consumers' Association lobbied and won statutory rights to consumer protection. In addition, it forced government to address legislation governing labelling and advertising of goods, credit agreements, guarantees and procedures for complaints and redress (Pfeffer and Coote, 1991).

The impact of the consumer movement on organisations is called *consumerism*: it led organisations to increase the quality of the goods and services that they offered or they went out of business, as customers demanded compensation for shoddy products and/or went elsewhere (Pfeffer and Coote, 1991; Sanderson, 1992). By the end of the 1980s organisations faced increasing demands from the general public for high-quality products and services. As a result, managers began to focus closely on the needs and wants of their customers.

In response to the expansion of the consumer movement into public services, the concept of the *Public Service Orientation* was developed and promoted by the work of Clarke and Stewart (1987) and the Local Government Training Board (LGTB) (1987). This concept was designed to encourage local authorities to address the needs of those using their services.

The Public Service Orientation is based on five principles:

- a local authority's activities are not carried out for their own sake, but to provide a service for the public;
- a local authority will be judged by the quality of service provided within the resources available;
- the service provided is only of real value if it is of value to those for whom it is provided;
- those for whom services are provided are customers demanding high-quality services and citizens entitled to receive it;
- quality of service demands closeness to the customer and the citizen.

(Local Government Training Board, 1987: p. 4)

As can be seen from the above principles, the underlying theme was a close focus on the customer and as a result of the Public Service Orientation, public services began to be designed and delivered to meet the needs of the public, rather than the authority itself. This change was described by the Local Government Training Board (1987) as a service *for* the customer, rather than *to* the customer.

This encouraged local authorities to pay close attention to the actual views, needs and wishes of the community and to build these into decision making. By the 1990s many managers were focusing on what customers wanted from their services and were using this to guide their management practice. In short, public sector organisations became customer-focused. This was further promoted by the development and launch of the 1991 Conservative Government's *Citizen's Charter*. This was introduced to make public services more accountable to the public and to raise the overall standards of provision. It aimed to improve quality, choice, standards and value in public services (HMSO, 1991). The Citizen's Charter is made up of seven principles of public service, which are:

- *standards:* local authorities have to set, monitor and publish explicit standards of performance;
- *openness:* full accurate information about how public services are run has to be provided, including the costs involved and performance levels obtained;
- *information*: full and accurate information on the services available has to be provided, written in plain language;
- *choice*: a choice of services has to be offered wherever possible;
- *non-discrimination*: local authority services should be available to all;
- *accessibility*: services should be run in order to be convenient for the customer;
- *redress*: a well-publicised and readily available procedure for compensation must be available.

The Citizen's Charter made it mandatory for public services to adhere to these principles in their everyday management and brought about increasing accountability to the public. This was because it forced managers to provide information on services, to collect data in order to monitor performance and increased the customer focus of public sector management. As a result, the Citizen's Charter promoted an increasing focus on customers and improved service delivery.

The impact of consumerism on public sport and leisure services was evidenced by increasing customer expectations of the range and quality of the services that were available. In response to this, managers began to introduce techniques that allowed them to become customer-focused in the delivery of their services. Many of the techniques were imported from the commercial sector and included:

- the direct collection of public views by customer surveys, focus groups and comments procedures;
- attempts to provide access to services through initiatives such as outreach work, community work and discount cards for low-income groups;
- increased access to information, predominantly in the form of leaflets and increased information outlets;
- the use of subjective indicators of performance, such as how customers felt about the leisure service;

- the use of techniques that improved the management of the service like quality management.
    (Leisure Futures, 1994; Nichols and Taylor, 1995; Robinson, 1999a)

The most significant response to consumerism was the development of customer care programmes, which focused on the major customer groups of sport and leisure services. Customer comment cards, market research and staff training gained prominence in the late 1980s as public sport and leisure managers responded to increasing customer expectations. Like the Public Service Orientation, this focus upon customers led to services that met the actual requirements of the customer, rather than their perceived requirements. This represented a change in attention from the service deliverer to the customer. Table 2.1 outlines the responses to consumerism made by six public sport and leisure providers. From this it is clear that consumerism has had a significant impact, promoting the use of the techniques associated with new managerialism.

Increasing competition

The second factor that has led to the emergence of new managerialism is increasing market competition. Mintel (2000) outlined how the value of the leisure industry increased by 23 per cent between 1994 and 1999, primarily as a result of capital expenditure on restaurants and pubs and cultural activities. In particular, they noted a 56 per cent increase in the leisure activities market during this period. For public managers, competition not only comes from local alternatives, but also from sport and leisure providers abroad. Luker (2000: p. 48), in his analysis of the sport industry, stated that:

> changing market places, new technology and fresh competition for the public leisure time and dollars means that old assumptions have to be challenged. . . . It's no longer about getting people to say yes to your sport – it's about getting people not to say no.

The increasingly competitive market for sport and leisure services is primarily due to improvements in technology. First, technological advances in means of travel have made customers far more mobile, allowing them to buy services in other cities, countries or even hemispheres. Second, modern communications have shrunk the sport and leisure world to little more than a village. It is possible for people to view music and sport events from all over the world, or have as their 'local' team a sports team in another country. 'Virtual' museums and galleries are becoming increasingly common, while the use of internet technology is a leisure activity in itself. For those who provide libraries, the impact of the World Wide Web has been even more significant as it provides information services that had previously been the domain of libraries.

Table 2.1 Responses to consumerism

	Use of customer surveys	Increase in information	Use of subjective performance indicators	Management techniques
King's Lynn and West Norfolk Borough Council	Customer comment cards Sports Forums User and non-user surveys	Publicised performance standards Service leaflets Facility leaflets Customer contract	Customer contract with service standards Measures of effectiveness from customer cards	Sport and Recreation Strategy Performance indicators Appraisal system Quality management
Warrington Council	Customer comments cards 'Are you being served' Suggestion schemes User surveys	Publicised performance standards Service leaflets Facility leaflets Customer contract	Customer contract with service standards	Service development plans Performance indicators Quality management
Erewash Borough Council	Complaints and suggestions scheme User surveys	Publicised performance standards Service leaflets Facility leaflets	Measurement of customer complaints Agreed service standards	Business plans Employee development reviews Performance indicators Quality management
Newcastle City Council	'Compliments, Suggestions and Complaints' Scheme Focus groups	Publicised performance standards Service leaflets Facility leaflets	Quality is a key result area Measurement of customer complaints	Service plans Performance indicators Staff surveys Quality management
Calderdale Council	Customer comments cards User forums User surveys	Publicised performance standards Service leaflets Facility leaflets Customer contract	Customer contract with service standards	Business plans Performance indicators Quality management
Scunthorpe Borough Council	Customer comment scheme User surveys	Publicised performance standards Service leaflets Facility leaflets	Has measures of effectiveness	Strategic planning Business planning Performance indicators Staff review scheme Quality management

Source: Robinson, 1999a.

Competitiveness becomes even more prominent when considering that providers compete for discretionary expenditure and time. Thus, managers are not only competing within the industry, but are also competing with other ways of using spare time and discretionary income. The opportunity for choice, which differentiates sport and leisure from most other public services, alongside the requirement to generate revenue for the local authority, reinforces the need for these services to be managed in an effective manner. Customers can choose whether to make use of the local authority service, they can choose which sport and leisure service to use and they can change their habits at any time. This requires a business approach to service delivery in order to ensure survival in an increasingly competitive industry.

Central government legislation

The third factor that has promoted the emergence of new managerialism is central government legislation, as changes in legislation affecting public sport and leisure service delivery have impacted significantly upon its management.

The general acceptance of local government as a 'good thing' began to erode in the mid-1970s and has declined ever since under both Conservative and Labour governments. Criticised for overspending and poor management, the mid-1970s saw local authorities enter a period of significant central government intervention in the management and service delivery, which has continued ever since. This was typified by the series of documents and papers released by the Audit Commission between 1986 and 1988 in which it argued that, in order to bring about greater accountability and spending restraint, local government needed to introduce a comprehensive system of performance review. The Audit Commission argued that local authorities should evaluate the effectiveness of their services, consider outcomes as well as inputs and outputs and monitor and review performance as a matter of course. It was felt that this process of performance review would address the management weaknesses that the Conservative Government thought to be inherent within local authorities. The government hostility towards local authorities was still clearly evident in the report *Performance Review in Local Government* released by the Audit Commission (1988: p. 1), nearly a decade later. Here it was stated that the continued existence of local government 'depends on its ability to be competitive, offer consumer choice and provide well-managed, quality services'. The underlying belief of central government was that the way the commercial sector was managed should be the model to be followed in the public sector.

A review of public sport and leisure services led to the same criticisms as those made of other public services. The Audit Commission (1989) identified several weaknesses in the management of public sport and leisure services, which they felt made the service inefficient. First, they felt that many local authorities were unclear about the aims of their leisure service and stressed the need to balance social and financial objectives. In the keynote report *Sport for Whom?*, the Audit Commission (1989: p. 2) noted that:

> objectives are rarely quantified and success or failure in meeting objectives rarely measured or monitored. It is easy to 'move the goalposts' and explain any unexpectedly high deficit by invoking social objectives.

Investment decisions were also considered to be poorly thought out, often leading to similar facilities being built next to each other in neighbouring authorities. The Commission also called for a greater co-ordination between authorities and alternative providers. The practice of price subsidy followed by most public sport and leisure services was challenged, as were the methods of monitoring performance. Again, the commercial sector model of strategic review, competition and improved co-ordination were suggested as the way forward. This model has formed the basis of the two major pieces of legislation that have affected public sport and leisure services: CCT and Best Value.

Compulsory competitive tendering

The belief in the commercial sector model of management provided the justification for the introduction of CCT, as the underlying premise of this initiative was that market competition would ensure efficient and cost-effective services, free from subsidy. Winners of CCT contracts were required to meet financially driven performance targets and budgets, while those responsible for the administration of the contracts were required to write objectives for the service and to monitor the performance of the contract. CCT was seen as a way of forcing local authorities to adopt the management techniques that had been promoted by the Audit Commission.

Despite the major changes required by the legislation, on completion of the first round of tendering in 1993 it appeared that the objective of compulsory competitive tendering had only been met in a limited fashion. There was little evidence that public sport and leisure services had been greatly opened up to competition. Research carried out by the Audit Commission (1993) showed that local authorities' Direct Service Organisations had won 82 per cent of sport and leisure management contracts. Many of these had been won uncontested. Commercial interest in sport and leisure provision was minimal, primarily because of the cost of running such facilities; of those contracts put out to tender in England only 18 per cent attracted three bids or more.

Although CCT did not initially appear to open up sport and leisure services to market competition, it did partially achieve its main goal as it can be argued that CCT became a catalyst for the commercialisation of management within leisure services. Certainly, the use of management techniques traditionally associated with the commercial sector became increasingly prevalent in public sport and leisure services after the introduction of CCT (Henry, 2001; Robinson, 1999b).

This was partly due to the tendering process itself, which forced local authorities to review their strategic and operational practices. In addition, the role of CCT in promoting the generation of management information was discussed by Nichols and Taylor (1995) and Nichols (1996), who concluded that compulsory competitive tendering was the catalyst for the generation of greater information on the costs of the service, levels of demand and the requirements of users. CCT also brought about improvements in the quality of services offered by public sport and leisure services and improved responsiveness to customers (Robinson, 1999a). Arguably therefore CCT would appear to have achieved its objective of making the management of public facilities more effective.

However, evidence of the impact of CCT on public sport and leisure services suggests that CCT had some serious negative impacts. First, the tendering process itself was costly. It required time for local authority officers to prepare the contract documents, assess potential bidders and then run the contract. The process of advertising and management of the contract was also financially costly. In addition, as most authorities tendered a bid to manage their facilities, they also had to bear the costs of preparing a tender. Second, staff morale and motivation suffered (Leisure Futures, 1994). One way of making financial savings was to cut back on the number of staff and the rewards used to motivate them. In addition, the possibility of job losses (if the contract was not won) had a detrimental effect. Third, although service quality improved in order to attract customers (Henry, 2001; Robinson, 1999a), the general fabric of facilities declined. Although contractors were required to maintain equipment, they were not required to maintain the buildings. Local authorities often failed to see why they should maintain a building that they were not responsible for managing. The consequence of this stand-off was a significant decline in the standards of public sport and leisure buildings.

Finally, and most important, CCT led to a decline in the importance of social objectives (Robinson, 2002; Stevens and Green, 2002). Contractors were required to meet the objectives outlined in the contract and in nearly all cases these were predominantly financial. Contractors were therefore unsurprisingly concerned with revenue generation and tended to ignore or down play those services that did not generate revenue. This led to a decline in focus on social objectives, as the services associated with social objectives do not tend to bring in revenue. As the rationale for the provision of public sport and leisure services is to provide services for all of the community, the decrease in importance placed on social objectives was clearly an undesirable consequence of the CCT legislation.

Best Value

Central government commitment to the commercialisation of public services continued with the advent of Labour Party control in 1997. Based on a performance management approach to service delivery that is outlined in Figure 2.2, Sanderson (1998: p. 6) has outlined how the programme of Best Value is 'firmly rooted in the corporate planning process through which a local authority identifies its objectives and priorities and the values that underpin them.' A significant difference between CCT and Best Value is that Best Value has to be applied to all types of leisure service, including those that had been exempt under CCT. In order to signify this change, the Best Value legislation refers to *cultural services,* which include museums, galleries, libraries and sport and leisure facilities.

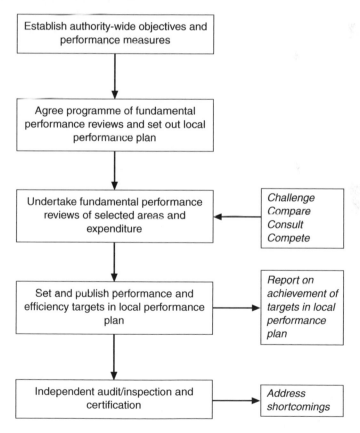

Figure 2.2 The Best Value performance management framework.
Source: Adapted from DETR, 1998a.

As outlined in Table 2.2, the impact of Best Value has been primarily positive. Research carried out by Davies and Girdler (2000) and Nichols and Robinson (2000) has shown that Best Value is encouraging market testing and that public sport and leisure providers are actively seeking partnerships to assist with the delivery of their services. In many cases, this is leading to investment in facilities, particularly if the public sector goes into partnership with the commercial sector. In addition, there has been a re-focus on the social objectives of sport and leisure and increased consultation to bring about increased accountability.

Compared to performance data for all service areas, the quality of sport and recreation services is high, with more services judged as excellent and no services judged as poor (Audit Commission, 2002). However, it is not all positive. The Audit Commission (2001) found that 55 per cent of the sport and recreation services that they audited were only judged as delivering a fair service, 39 per cent were delivering a good service and 6 per cent were delivering an excellent service. The auditors of sport and recreation facilities felt that managers needed to pay closer attention to the purpose and priorities of the service in terms of their councils' objectives; they needed to consider more appropriate delivery mechanisms and to take more practical steps towards improving services (Audit Commission, 2002). This suggests that managers need to continue to invest time in the use of techniques to improve service delivery.

From this it is clear that central government legislation has facilitated, and continues to facilitate, the emergence of new managerialism, particularly with the advent of Comprehensive Performance Assessment as outlined in Chapter 1. Policy initiatives over the past two decades, from two different political parties, have promoted the use of commercial management techniques in order to meet the demands of the legislation. Alongside the impact of consumerism and market competition, this has led managers to ensure that new managerialism is firmly entrenched within the management of public sport and leisure services.

Table 2.2 Summary of the performance of the different public services

	% of users satisfied	% judged as good/ excellent	% probably/ will improve
Housing	54–77	23	56
Environment	62–78 (waste) 39–47 (highways)	41	52
Culture and Leisure	72–88 (culture) 63–82 (leisure)	41	47
Corporate	63–67 (revenue)	34	50
Social services	55–74	26	68
Education	70–80	68	na

Source: Adapted from Audit Commission, 2001.

The public sport and leisure context

Over the last two decades, the three factors outlined above (consumerism, increasing competition and government legislation) have interacted to bring about changes in the management style of public sport and leisure services. Managers, having identified the importance of responding to these factors, introduced management techniques that have traditionally been associated with the commercial sector. As a result, there is now little apparent difference between the styles of management adopted by public managers and those adopted by commercial managers. What is different, however, is the context within which public sport and leisure managers work.

There are four important factors in the public context that have an impact on the way that managers can run their services. The first and most significant factor is that public sport and leisure services are part of a political system. This means they are guided and directed by the policies of both central and local government. Second, public providers are accountable to members of the public in a manner that commercial managers are not. Third, and closely associated with the above two factors, is the number of stakeholders that public sport and leisure services have, all with a vested interest in the running of the service. Finally, public sport and leisure managers are required to deliver services that meet dual, and often conflicting, objectives relating to operational and social priorities.

Political influences

Central government control of local authorities stems from the principle of 'ultra vires', which was established by the 1835 Municipal Corporations Act. As a consequence, local authorities are:

> literally the creatures, the creations of parliamentary statute. Their boundaries, duties, powers, memberships and modes of operation are laid down by Acts of Parliament.
>
> (Wilson and Game, 1994: p. 23)

They are therefore intrinsically affected by the policies and legislation of Westminster.

Central government dictates the structure of local government, allocates finances, and lays out how local authorities should be run. Local authorities are told what services must be delivered and what services they have a choice about delivering. Furthermore, central government audits local government and can take over the running of services if these are deemed to be badly run. As a result, public sport and leisure services are required to implement the policies and legislation promoted by central government, even if this requires a complete restructure of the service, as in the case of

CCT, or the end of contractual arrangements, as brought about by Best Value.

To a lesser extent, managers are also influenced by the politics of their local councils. Local political interests will affect the objectives to be achieved by the service or may influence investment decisions. For example, local politicians may adopt a policy of heavily subsidising the cost of sport and leisure opportunities in order to keep fees low, despite the fact that many of those who use the facilities can afford to pay much more. Managers do not have to agree with the policies affecting their services, they simply have to implement them in the most effective way possible.

Accountability to the public

As political organisations, public sport and leisure services are ultimately accountable to the public that they serve. This is for two reasons. First, the provision, or lack of provision, of sport and leisure services affects the quality of life for people in the local area. As a result, members of public wish to understand the decision-making process that influences the delivery of leisure services and the outcome of this process. Second, and more importantly, public services are funded out of taxes that people either pay to central government or directly to the local authority in the form of council tax. Those who pay these taxes will obviously be concerned that their money is being used in the most efficient and effective manner. Managers are required to demonstrate this by publishing performance targets and accounting for the performance against these targets (see Chapters 4 and 7). Commercial leisure managers do not have this accountability. Although some will be required by law to publish company accounts, there is no requirement to openly publish and discuss the performance of the organisation.

Stakeholders

Stakeholders are those people or groups who have a vested interest in the way that services are managed and operated. Commercial organisations have a limited number of stakeholders – users, staff and shareholders – whereas, due to the nature of local authorities, public sport and leisure providers have a range of stakeholders, including:

- the direct user of the service, such as a borrower at a library;
- the person who benefits from the service without directly using the service, such as parents whose children attend holiday activity programmes;
- councillors and local politicians;
- funding bodies, such as Sport England;

- community residents;
- council taxpayers.

The number of stakeholders relevant to public sport and leisure services causes difficulties for the managers of these services. Each of these stakeholder groups and, indeed, people within these groups, may have a different expectation of the way the service should be managed and the services that should be delivered. Public accountability for sport and leisure services differs from many other local authority services, as those who pay council tax can choose whether they use the service or not. This creates a group of non-using stakeholders who are more likely to be concerned with the cost of provision, rather than the content or quality of the service provided. This is likely to conflict with the requirements of those who actually use the service.

Objectives

Public sport and leisure providers are required to deliver services that meet two sets of objectives. The first set are operational, concerned with such areas as costs, staff turnover, programming and revenue generation. Local authorities, however, have a second set of social objectives. These objectives are more esoteric and, unlike operational objectives, tend to lack clarity, which makes them a poor guide for service delivery. In addition, measurement of performance against such objectives is problematic as it is often difficult to define a direct outcome as a result of trying to achieve social objectives.

Commercial leisure services tend to operate under less complex and less disputed goals. The provision of services to meet social objectives is not an issue that greatly influences the commercial sector. Although there is increasing concern among commercial providers with environmental impacts, ultimately they justify their continued existence on their ability to meet market forces.

Summary and conclusions

This chapter has described the development of new managerialism, a style of management that is prevalent within public sport and leisure services. The impact of consumerism, market competition and government legislation has led to these services being managed in a way that is similar to that of commercial services. The context within which public managers work is, however, different. The political environment within which services operate, the need to be accountable to the public and other stakeholders and to deliver social objectives makes public sport and leisure management distinctly different and more complex than that of the commercial sector. The environment in which public sector leisure services are delivered requires managers to be able to account for their performance in both financial and social terms. As the commercial sector does not usually have to justify its performance in social terms, it can be argued that public sport and leisure managers now have a more demanding job than their commercial sector counterparts.

Further reading

Institute of Sport and Recreation Management (2000) *Best Value Review: The essential tool kit for today's managers of local authority sport and recreation service*, Melton Mowbray: ISRM.

3 Managing public sport and leisure services

Management is a formal process that occurs within organisations in order to direct and organise resources to meet stated objectives. Mullins (1996: p. 398) regards management as:

- taking place within a structured organisational setting with prescribed roles;
- directed towards the attainment of aims and objectives;
- achieved through the efforts of other people;
- using systems and procedures.

This chapter introduces the functions of management in the public sport and leisure sector. It describes appropriate management styles and considers the skills necessary for effective management. It is, however, important to note that the skills discussed below are essential for the managers of all sport and leisure services, no matter what sector their organisation is operating within. These skills then need to be applied to the specific sector context in order to be most effective and examples of how to do this in the public sector will be given. The chapter ends with a discussion of the issues that affect management by considering culture, politics and power.

Introduction

Understanding management and what managers do in organisations has been and remains the focus of intensive research. This is because managers have the ability to fundamentally affect the success of an organisation through their approach to staff, resources and customers. Consideration of the research cited below suggests that there are five approaches to understanding the way that management operates. These are:

- the classical approach (Taylor, 1972; Fayol, 1967): this approach is based on the premise that there is core knowledge that managers should have in order to carry out their role, such as the ability to plan and organise;

- the behavioural approach (Follet, 1924; Mayo, 1933): this suggests that individuals should be the focus of management, which should address individual needs and wants;
- the management science approach: this approach is concerned with rational solving of problems and is based on the premise that there is a 'right' way of doing things;
- the systems approach (Katz and Kahn, 1966): this suggests that there is a system of management that is made up of a number of parts that all need to come together to achieve organisational objectives;
- the contingency approach (Burns and Stalker, 1961; Fiedler, 1967; Lawrence and Lorsh, 1967): this is based on the assumption that there is no single way of managing, rather managers need to be flexible in order to respond to different situations.

(Adapted from Watt, 1998; Rees and Porter, 2001)

It is this last approach that is the most appropriate for sport and leisure services, as managers need to be able to adopt styles of management that allow them to deal with politicians, funding bodies, different categories of staff, customers and a range of service issues.

The contingency approach to management

The basic premise of contingency theory is that there is no one style of management that is appropriate for all situations. One of the best known contingency theories is the 'best fit' approach (Handy, 1993) that suggests that in any situation there are a number of influencing factors that a manager must take into consideration:

- their operating style as a manager: most managers will have a preferred style of managing which means that they will have a natural way of reacting when under stress. They need to be aware of the strengths and limitations of this style;
- the preferred style of their staff: in order to gain loyalty and respect, a manager needs to be able to manage in a style appropriate for their staff. Staff are likely to have a preferred way of being managed. For example, usually new staff and younger staff will feel more comfortable with strong guidance. Conversely, senior staff or experienced staff are likely to be more comfortable with participating in decision making or having work delegated to them;
- the task: the task itself will dictate how a manager should act. If it is a simple task, a discussion about how to undertake the task is inappropriate. The manager should either tell staff what can be done or delegate the task. Alternatively, a complex task that will have a significant impact on staff must be managed through consultation and discussion;
- the environment: the organisation itself will affect style. Some organi-

sations, such as the armed services or emergency services do not particularly encourage a style of management that emphasises consultation with staff as often decisions need to be made instantaneously. Other organisations will allow a range of styles to be adopted, in order to suit the variety of issues a manager has to deal with.

The need for flexibility in the management of public sport and leisure services is reinforced when considering the number of roles that a manager has within an organisation.

The roles of management

The role of a manager is varied and complex. Research carried out by Mintzberg (1979) led him to suggest that managers have ten roles to play within organisations. He further organised these roles into three main sets as outlined in Table 3.1.

Table 3.1 Managerial roles

Inter-personal roles	
Figurehead	The manager acts as the representative of the organisation, such as attending industry meetings or giving out staff achievement awards
Leader	The manager is concerned with the relationships between staff, what motivates them and what needs they may have
Liaison	The manager networks/works with others outside the organisation or department
Information roles	
Monitor	This requires managers to monitor the internal and external environment in order to stay up to date with changes
Disseminator	The manager has the responsibility to pass on information within the organisation. They have a duty to keep staff informed
Spokesperson	The manager gives information about the organisation, to others outside the organisation
Decisional roles	
Entrepreneur	This role requires managers to be innovative and to be able to introduce and manage change
Disturbance handler	The manager has to be able to resolve problems and handle conflict
Resource allocator	All managers have to control and distribute resources
Negotiator	All managers will have to negotiate and debate issues in order to successfully allocate resources and meet objectives

Source: Mintzberg, 1979.

A point worth noting is that Mintzberg, along with many others (Handy, 1993; Hersey *et al.*, 1996; Watt, 1998), separates management from leadership. He considers leadership to be one aspect of a manager's job, a view supported by Handy (1993), who feels that leading is primarily concerned with the interpersonal activities of a manager's job. Although there are various explanations of the differences between management and leadership, there is a general consensus that leadership is about the ability to influence others in the pursuit of organisational goals. This means that although all managers should be able to lead, not all leaders will be managers, as leadership is not necessarily related to position in the organisation. This point will be discussed further in this chapter and in Chapter 9.

The skills of management

The management of public sport and leisure services requires a number of skills. Gilgeous (1997) has suggested that these skills can be classified into four main categories, which are

- general management skills, such as communication, decision making and conflict management;
- personal characteristics, such as leadership, enthusiasm, flexibility and fairness;
- functional management skills, such as marketing or finance;
- industry-specific skills, such as coaching.

Although managers are unlikely to possess all of the skills to be discussed below, they must have abilities in each of the above categories in order to be effective.

General management skills

There are a number of skills that managers need, no matter what their role is in the public sport and leisure service. Those who manage facilities, run outreach programmes or are responsible for the entire service require the skills outlined below.

Decision making

Management is all about making decisions. Decisions need to be made regarding the allocation of resources, the future direction of the service or the colour of staff uniforms. To make rational decisions, managers need to be clear about the choices available and the criteria against which the choice should be made. They then need to obtain sufficient information in order to assess the choices against these criteria and use this to come to a decision. Figure 3.1 outlines the rational approach to decision making, highlighting the process that managers should go through.

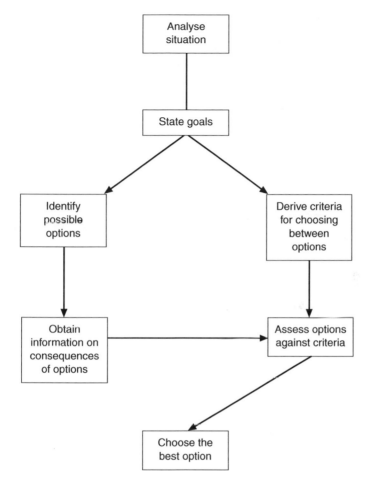

Figure 3.1 The rational approach to decision making.

Source: Adapted from Batsleer, 1994.

However, managerial decision making rarely follows this process and managers make decisions based on a range of factors such as past experience, judgement, creativity and personal abilities. Decisions are usually made under time constraints and without comprehensive information. Therefore decision making is rarely rational. In fact, in most cases managers aim to make the best possible or most satisfactory decision under the circumstances. Known as *satisficing* (March and Simon, 1958), managers seek solutions that are good enough, rather than being the optimal solution to a problem. This leads to the process of bounded decision making as outlined in Figure 3.2.

Using this approach, managers try out solutions that have worked in

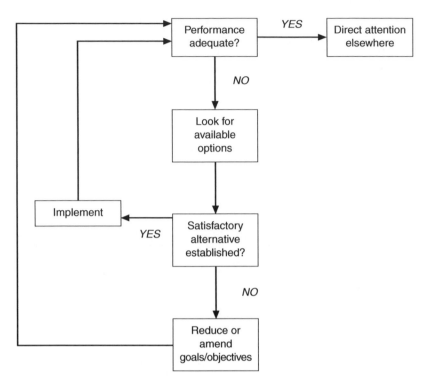

Figure 3.2 The bounded approach to decision making.

Source: Adapted from Batsleer, 1994.

the past, or that they are aware have been successful for other organisations, colleagues or departments. If none of these work, managers either reduce their expectations or will eventually move on to the rational process, where they will seek information and evaluate options. Although bounded decision making is arguably less effective than rational decision making, it does allow managers to make the best of their limited time and to deal with as many issues as possible.

There are three types of conditions under which decisions are made. First, decisions can be made under conditions of *certainty*, when the manager is aware of all of the alternatives and is clear about the outcomes of making a particular decision. However, as a result of the environment within which public sport and leisure managers work, they can never be sure of the exact consequences of decisions they make, even if they follow a process of rational decision making. Thus, managers are unlikely to make many decisions about which they are certain. Second, decisions can also be made under the condition of risk; that is, the manager has an idea of the choices available, but no definite idea of the outcomes of the choices. Thus, there is a risk to making a decision and managers usually collect additional information to reduce the risk, or make a choice based on their previous experience (bounded). Finally, decisions can be made under conditions of uncertainty, where there is no clear idea of the alternatives and therefore the outcomes (Jones *et al.*, 1998). This does not happen often, but does arise in situations where there has been no precedent. Uncertainty can be reduced by gathering additional information about the issue.

Clearly decisions made under conditions of certainty are the safest for managers and the organisation. However, as managers have very few opportunities to make such decisions, they should try to reduce the risk of decision making, particularly for significant issues, such as a decision about investment in facilities or services. Torkildsen (1999) has suggested a nine-step approach to ensuring that decision making is as effective as possible. He suggests that managers should:

- define the problem: managers need to be clear about exactly what the problem is. It is often easy to confuse the symptoms of the problem with the problem itself; for example, trying to deal with customer dissatisfaction in general, rather than establishing what has caused it;
- gather and examine information and identify possible causes of the problem;
- consult with others: other people may have a different perspective on an issue and by seeking the opinions of others a better solution may be identified;
- consider choices and alternatives;
- consider the implications of the choices: some decisions may solve the problem, but will cause greater problems. For example, closing a swimming pool will make a significant financial saving, but will lead to a loss of customer goodwill and will increase customer dissatisfaction;
- make the decision;
- communicate the decision: the decision must be unambiguous, communicated clearly and appropriately and managers must be prepared to be able to convince other people that the decision is correct;
- implement and follow up the decision;
- evaluate the impact of the decision and modify the decision if necessary.

This is clearly a lengthy process and is not likely to occur for all decision making, indeed it is not appropriate for all decisions. It is important, however, that the risk is reduced in decision making when the decisions are of such significance that they can fundamentally affect the organisation and/or staff working within it.

Communication

The ability to communicate is arguably the most important skill required of managers (Jones *et al.*, 1998; Rees and Porter, 2001). Communication aims to influence understanding, attitudes and behaviour and is concerned with the passing on and receiving of information. This allows managers to manage staff, make decisions, carry out planning and solve problems. Communication must be clear, frequent and involve everyone.

Jones *et al.* (1998) have highlighted a number of advantages to good communication. First, it increases efficiency, since staff make fewer mistakes when they are clear about what tasks have to be achieved, why they have to be completed and how to go about these tasks. Not only is this beneficial in terms of motivating staff, it also reduces costs to the organisation as fewer errors are made. Second, quality is improved by good communication as managers should be able to communicate the meaning and importance of good quality and the routes to obtaining it. Third, customer responsiveness is contingent on the ability of managers to establish what customers need and pass this on to the organisation. Finally, greater employee motivation and involvement and reduction of mistakes result in better service to the customer.

There are several ways of communicating information and managers are likely to spend most of their time engaged in some form of communication process. The choice of communication method will depend on three main factors. First, the purpose of the communication will affect the way the information should be communicated. Information in writing tends to be more formal than that offered verbally. For example, an offer of employment must be made in writing, while an offer of additional training could be made verbally. Second, the target audience needs to be considered. It is appropriate to carry out staff briefings verbally, for example, whereas customer newsletters will be written. In addition, information needs to be delivered in a language appropriate for the target audience. This may mean that information has to be delivered in a foreign language, in large print or even in pictures if trying to communicate with children. Finally, the length of the communication is important. Short messages are appropriate for verbal methods, while lengthy and complex information is better disseminated in writing, so that people can return to it to complete their understanding.

The ability to listen is also an essential communication tool for a manager (Hersey *et al.*, 1996; Pearce, 1993). Managers must hear and understand the information that is been passed on, rather than just focusing on the words that are being said. Unfortunately, hearing is often easier than listening and research carried out by Rogers (1951) developed the concept of *active listening*, a term that covers those characteristics that ensure that managers hear and understand the information that they are being given. Although the process outlined below is not appropriate for all situations, active listening allows managers to demonstrate that they are interested in what is being said and that they have heard and understood the message. Active listening is particularly appropriate for appraisal interviews, or discipline and grievance interviews (see Chapter 5) or when counselling members of staff.

Rogers (1951) proposed five parts to active listening. First, the manager must listen for the content of the message by making an effort to hear precisely what is being said. Second, the manager must listen for the feelings of the speaker and try and perceive what is actually being said through the way the message is being delivered. Third, these feelings need a response and managers need to demonstrate that they recognise and understand how the speaker is feeling. Fourth, the manager must note the verbal and non-verbal cues that are being given off to check for mixed messages. Finally, the manager must reflect on what has been said, by paraphrasing the information back to the speaker to show that they have understood. This process will allow managers to make more informed decisions or will encourage staff to make their own decisions.

Managing conflict

Conflict between individuals and teams is a part of every organisation (Jones *et al.*, 1998). Individuals and teams compete for financial resources, time from managers, equipment and even customers and this competition will, on occasions, result in conflict within the organisation. Conflict within organisations is not always a bad thing and constructive conflict can serve a variety of functions. First, it can encourage people to work together to fight a common enemy. Second, it can help to define roles and increase understanding of the feelings of others in the team. Finally, constructive conflict can increase understanding of the issues involved, as conflict usually arises when individuals are not aware of the concerns of all involved. Alternatively, destructive conflict is usually detrimental to the organisation as it tends to be based on personality differences or is concerned with the preservation of power. Managers need to be able to identify destructive conflict and have a strategy for dealing with it.

Research carried out by Thomas (1976) suggests that there are a number of ways of dealing with conflict and the appropriate strategy often depends on the reason why the conflict has arisen. For example, if conflict has arisen because of competition for resources, an increase in available resources will end or reduce the conflict. In addition, the strategy adopted to handle the conflict will depend on the style adopted by the manager when dealing with it. Much the same as the contingency style of management, there is no correct way of handling conflict and managers should be able to adopt any one of the styles outlined below:

- competing: this creates a situation where the conflict will be resolved to suit one of the parties only;

- collaborating: in this situation both parties gain as they work together to come to a solution;
- compromising: the needs of both parties are partially satisfied as this strategy requires both to reduce their claims;
- avoiding: this occurs when the manager ignores the conflict or deflects attention away from it. The only advantage to this strategy is that it may allow a cooling-off period as the two parties focus on other issues;
- accommodating: in this situation only one party will be successful, but the process is handled in such a manner that both parties are relatively satisfied.

Table 3.2 outlines when each style may be appropriate.

There are a number of issues to be considered before tackling conflict. The first question to be addressed is whether it is worth intervening. If the conflict is not affecting the work of those involved and looks like it will resolve itself, the intervention of a manager may inflame the situation. The decision of whether to intervene or not will be assisted by being clear about what has caused the conflict and the significance of the issue. Managers must also have the personality characteristics and communication skills to be able to deal with the conflict in a calm, rational and fair manner. If they lack these skills, it is often better that someone else deals with the situation. Finally, the timing of the intervention is important. Managers must intervene at a time when they can actually be of use, rather than too early or too late when intervention may escalate the conflict or inflame it.

Once the decision has been made to intervene, a strategy to deal with the situation is required. Managers should:

- identify the problem: this requires them to identify who is involved in the conflict, why this conflict has arisen and the issues involved;
- examine the relationships that the protagonists have within the organisations: this will allow managers to identify other people who may help to resolve the problem;
- identify the problems and the costs of the behaviour: this may be in terms of time wasted, the demotivating effect on others in the team, or an unpalatable atmosphere;
- approach those involved in the conflict and work together to search for a solution;
- implement the solution and then evaluate the situation on an ongoing basis until sure that the conflict has ended.

Although handling conflict is often an unpleasant task, if it is ignored there are likely to be negative consequences for the organisation. The best strategy is to be aware of where conflict may arise and to set in place plans

Table 3.2 Situations in which to use the conflict-handling styles

Competing	When quick, decisive action is vital
	On important actions where unpopular actions need implementing, such as making cuts in budgets
	On issues vital to the organisation, when the manager knows that he or she is right
	When dealing with people who take advantage of non-competitive behaviour
Collaborating	To find an integrative solution when both sets of concerns are too important to be compromised
	When the objective is to learn
	To merge insights from people with different perspectives
	To gain commitment by incorporating concerns into a consensus
	To work through feelings which have interfered with a relationship
Compromising	When goals are important, but not worth the effort or potential disruption of more assertive modes of handling conflict
	When opponents with equal power are committed to mutually exclusive goals
	To achieve temporary settlements to complex issues
	To arrive at expedient solutions to complex issues
	As a back up when collaboration or competition is unsuccessful
Avoiding	When an issue is trivial or more important issues are pressing
	When you perceive no chance of satisfying your concerns
	When potential disruption outweighs the benefits of resolution
	To let people cool down and gain perspective
	When gathering information supersedes an immediate decision
	When issues seem tangential or symptomatic of other issues
Accommodating	When you find out you are wrong – to allow a better position to be heard, to learn, to show your reasonableness
	When issues are more important to others than to yourself – to satisfy others and maintain cooperation
	To build social credits for later issues
	To minimise loss when you are outmatched and losing
	When harmony and stability are especially important
	To allow subordinates to develop by learning from mistakes

Source: Thomas, 1976.

to prevent it from arising. This is not, however, always possible and, once identified, conflict needs to be managed in an efficient and effective manner.

Delegation

Delegation is the process of giving a subordinate additional responsibility for a certain task *and* the authority to get the job done, whilst retaining overall control (Rees and Porter, 2001). As an important part of staff development it gives staff the opportunity to learn new skills and take on extra responsibilities with the guidance of their manager.

Good delegation depends on a number of factors (Gilgeous, 1997). First, there must be tasks that are appropriate to be delegated. These need to be tightly defined, with clear objectives, but challenging enough for staff to be motivated by doing the task. Second, staff must have the skills to do the delegated task, or must be offered training in order to develop these skills. Third, managers will need good personal skills, in order to be able to explain the task, provide support when requested, but also to be able to leave the staff member to do the work. Finally, the organisation itself must be accepting of delegation. There is little point in delegating work to members of staff if the organisation will not allow them the authority to do the task, or reward them for having done it.

Delegation of work has many benefits. It is often necessary to ensure that the range of work for which managers have responsibility is carried out. It enables managers to concentrate on the key aspects of their job as defined by their personal objectives and as outlined above, provides an opportunity to extend the skills and experience of other staff. As a result, it acts as a motivating factor and increases morale. More importantly, it ensures that the work is done.

Despite these benefits, many managers are poor at delegating work and Rees and Porter (2001) identified two main reasons for this. First, some managers think that they are the only person who can do the work, and second, managers often feel that they do not have the time to train the staff member who could be doing the work. Delegation is initially time-consuming as staff need to be shown or trained to be able to carry out the additional work. Staff need to be clear about what has to be done, why it has to be done and when by. In addition, as they first tackle the task they will invariably be slower at it than a competent person. However, after this initial slowness, with appropriate support, staff will be as effective as the manager at the delegated task.

In addition, delegation requires some relinquishing of control and many managers find this difficult, particularly as they still remain ultimately accountable for the work. However, managers who are effective delegators demonstrate confidence in the abilities of the staff member and let them know that they are available for advice and guidance. Finally, it is important to let other people know what responsibility and authority has been given. If these principles are followed, delegation will become an important technique for managing the workload of managers.

Time management

Managing time is one of the problems of being a successful manager (Jones *et al.*, 1998). Managers often find it difficult to say 'no' to additional work, particularly if it appears of value to their team or themselves. However, if time is not managed properly, managers run the risk of being unable to complete their work to the standards they would like. Alternatively, they may become so overburdened that not all work can be completed. The pressure of time is exacerbated for sport and leisure managers as some of their work takes place during anti-social hours, such as evenings and weekends. This is because these periods of time are leisure time for most individuals and therefore organisations that provide sport and leisure services need to be managed during these hours. This creates more time pressure for managers, as evening and weekend work will conflict with the demands of their own home life, social activities and sport pursuits. The management of time becomes even more important as time lost in normal working hours cannot be caught up. Managers therefore need to be skilled at time management.

In order to have the time to do the work required, managers must have a time-management strategy. First, however, they need to be aware of the activities that cause time to be lost. These activities include:

- a lack of preparation: not spending enough time prioritising tasks or being clear about what has to be achieved;
- procrastination: putting off tasks that have to be achieved because they are too difficult or boring;
- poor prioritisation: working on tasks that are simple rather than important;
- confusing what is urgent with what is important: responding to the person who 'shouts the loudest' rather than doing the most important task;
- poor delegation: trying to do everything, rather than getting someone to assist, or delegating so poorly that the staff member has to continuously ask for help;
- poor communication: giving out incorrect or poorly expressed information so that time is wasted by having to provide more information or correcting errors that have come about as a result of poor information;
- lengthy phone calls, meetings or conversations: these often take longer than is required because the purpose is not clear or information is missing;

- taking work home after a full day: this is inefficient because of tiredness or conflicts with other demands.

(Adapted from Rees and Porter, 2001)

Once time-wasting activities have been identified, a time-management strategy should be formed, based on four principles. First, managers must record all commitments, including meetings, tasks to be completed and deadlines. They must carry out regular work planning and record this to ensure that plans are followed. Second, managers need to be clear about what it is that they have to achieve. It is not possible to do everything, so managers need to assess the tasks that are required of them in terms of what is necessary to achieve the objectives of their job. This will allow them to prioritise the tasks they have been asked to complete. It is easy to get sidetracked and to waste time on things that are interesting, but not essential. Third, managers need to structure their time. Time needs to be divided into blocks and allocated to certain activities. Tasks requiring concentration and research should be allocated to the time when the manager feels at their most alert. Alternatively, responding to phone calls, paperwork and e-mail can be left for times when concentrated work is less possible. In addition, it is important to identify time periods when managers can and cannot be disturbed by those who work with them. Finally, and most important, managers need to learn to say 'no'. Rather than making a manager appear lazy, the ability to turn down requests for work when overloaded or faced with other priorities, is an indication of efficiency.

Managers will, over time, develop time-management strategies that work best for them. Different techniques, such as delegation, using a 'To do' list or working from home, will suit different occupations, management styles and organisations (Quick and Quick, 1984). The key point to remember is that once time has been lost, it is impossible to make it up.

All of the skills outlined above are necessary for the effective management of public sport and leisure services. The ability to make decisions and communicate these and to organise and complete a full work load is required of all managers. Fortunately, all of these skills can be developed or improved by personal development activities, such as training courses. Therefore it is important for managers to evaluate their level of skill in the above areas and then improve on this if necessary.

Personal characteristics

The issue of personality traits and management has always been contentious as it implies that some people will be better managers simply because of their personality, rather than because of any learned knowledge or abilities. The contingency approach to management suggests that style is more important than personality; however, there are personal characteristics that can be considered to be essential for effective management. These are:

- consistency: the ability to be consistent in decision making and in the management of staff;
- decisiveness: the ability to make a decision;
- diplomacy: the ability to be subtle and tactful when dealing with others;
- enthusiasm: demonstrating keenness and eagerness about the work to be done;
- fairness: the possession of a sense of fair play and the ability not to 'take sides';
- flexibility: the ability to adapt and respond to change;
- honesty: being trustworthy, truthful and ethical;
- leadership: the ability to influence and guide others;
- self-confidence: being confident of decisions and actions;
- self-control: the ability to be calm and controlled in all situations.
    (Adapted from Gilgeous, 1997; Jones *et al.*, 1998; Thomson, 1997)

The level at which these characteristics naturally occur will vary: indeed, some may appear to be absent. However, like general management skills, it is possible to learn to adopt these characteristics. It is therefore, once again, important that managers are aware of their level of ability with respect to these characteristics and, if necessary, that they seek personal development activities to ensure they are making the best use of their individual characteristics.

Functional management skills

Most organisations, particularly those that are the size of local authorities, are split into separate functions, or departments. This allows staff within these departments to become experts within their chosen function, the premise being that they will then be in a position to advise other staff and departments on their particular function. The main functional areas in local authorities are finance, strategic planning, legal, human resources and marketing, and local authorities will have departments that deal with these functions of management.

Despite this, managers must have skills and knowledge in these areas. There are two reasons for this. First, these functions need to be applied to the sport and leisure context in order for them to be most effective for service management. It is likely that this will need to be done by service professionals as staff in the local authority department are unlikely to have as detailed a knowledge of the context as a sport and leisure manager. Second, in order to manage the performance of the service, managers need to understand all of the operations and activities affecting their service.

This requires them to know how the service is financed, how it is performing, how to recruit appropriate personnel and how to manage the quality of the service. Indeed, at a minimum, they need skills in the functions outlined in the following section of the book.

Industry-specific skills

This category of skills is needed to integrate and apply the above skills to the context of public sport and leisure provision. Managers may have technical knowledge of how to operate and maintain facilities and equipment and the ability to coach. However, the ability to advise on sport and leisure and to apply generic management skills successfully to the public sector makes managers distinct from those who run other services.

The technical skills associated with the industry are, however, less important than the abilities outlined above. It is not particularly necessary for a manager to be able to take a 'Learn To Swim' session or to set up equipment, although this may bestow credibility with staff. It is the ability to apply good management principles to the public sport and leisure industry, alongside an awareness of how public organisations operate that is important, as these are required for public sport and leisure managers to be effective.

Issues affecting the management of public sport and leisure services

The possession of the skills discussed above will improve the effectiveness of managers within the public sport and leisure service. There are, however, factors that will affect the way that managers can operate. This section looks at the impact of culture, power and politics on the management of these services.

Organisational culture

Organisational culture has been defined as:

> the basic assumptions and beliefs that are shared by members of an organisation, that operate unconsciously and that define in a basic 'taken-for-granted' fashion an organisation's view of itself and its environment.
>
> (Schein, 1985: p. 6)

Organisational culture shapes the organisation's goals and objectives, specifies the relationships that exist within the organisation and defines the valued qualities. It also outlines the accepted ways of working, acceptable behaviours and even acceptable dress (Handy, 1993; Schein, 1985). It is the way things are done in an organisation and therefore has a significant impact on the way that managers can manage public sport and leisure services.

Knowledge of culture comes about via knowledge of three aspects of the organisation (Schein, 1985; Slack, 1997). First, knowledge of the *shared tacit assumptions* of the organisation will be a key to its culture. For example, do people genuinely believe that is it acceptable to work from home or that customers are the focus of the organisation? It is often difficult to establish these shared assumptions, so a second source of information about culture is the *espoused values* of the organisation. In this case, managers could study strategic documentation and look at organisational priorities to try to identify how important the customer is or how flexible working arrangements are. If the organisation has a policy on home working or customer care, managers can get a feel for the organisation's values in these two areas. Third, organisational culture can be established by considering the *artefacts*, or the physical manifestations of the culture. For example, if a receptionist continues to talk to a colleague when there are customers waiting, the organisation does not value customers. Notices on office doors stating that staff are working from home suggests that this is something that is culturally acceptable. Culture is manifest in organisations in a number of ways and these are outlined in Table 3.3.

When considering public sport and leisure services, it is clear that the culture of these services is typified by the style of new managerialism, discussed in Chapter 2. This style, with its focus on customers and commitment to the use of good management techniques suggests that the culture

Table 3.3 Manifestations of organisational culture

Stories and myths	These are the stories that circulate in the organisation about incidents that have gone on in the past. Some of these may be true, but many are either untrue or have been exaggerated
Symbols	Logos, letterheads or mascots that are used to convey an image about the organisation
Language	The way that people speak to each other, the tone of printed material, how much jargon is used and the acronyms that are common within the organisation
Ceremonies or rites	The types of behaviour that occur within the organisation on a regular basis to achieve a certain purpose
Physical structure	The way the organisation is laid out in terms of access or the working environment
Artefacts	These are the physical evidence of culture

Source: Slack, 1997.

can be described as customer orientated and professional in its values. Evidence of this is found by considering many of the artefacts outlined in Table 3.3 and Table 3.4 provides examples of these artefacts from the public context.

An understanding of culture is important for managers as it impacts on decision making by affecting how resources are allocated and by suggesting what can and cannot be changed in the organisation. In addition, culture provides an explanation for why certain decisions are made, why some groups appear more important to the organisation than others and why some staff are promoted and others are not. Managers must therefore (first) understand culture and (second) use this understanding as a framework for their management activities. This will make them more effective within the organisation.

Power

Despite the vast body of academic literature considering power in organisations, there is no generally accepted definition of power. One definition of power that has been offered defines it as the ability of one person or group A to get another person or group B to do what A wants (Robins, 1994). This implies that power is not possessed, but manifests itself in terms of relationships with others and as a result, power within organisations is not fixed.

Table 3.4 Manifestations of the public sport and leisure service culture

Stories and myths	Stories about the impact of CCT or about the value of decisions made by councillors
Symbols	The use of logos associated with quality programmes to demonstrate that the service delivered is of a high quality The use of logos on all posters, pamphlets and advertising, which suggests professionalism and a corporate image
Language	First names are frequently used even when addressing seniors, which indicates a team approach The use of acronyms such as CCT and DDA (Disability Discrimination Act) indicates that there are issues that are so well-known that they can be referred to in shorthand
Ceremonies or rites	Staff annual parties that built team spirit or induction programmes that aim to incorporate new staff into the culture
Physical structure	The ease of customer access to reception indicates whether customers are important The use of lighting and CCTV cameras to instil a feeling of security
Artefacts	Uniforms, cleanliness, posters or lockers

Organisational power is considered to come from a number of sources, which are outlined below:

- physical: power comes from physical characteristics such as size, intelligence or looks. Strong people have physical power over weaker people as they are able to use their physical power to force the weaker person to do what is wanted. From an individual perspective, the exertion of physical power is inappropriate within organisations, although harassment and bullying unfortunately occurs within public sport and leisure services, as in any other field. From an organisational perspective, a larger organisation will have more resources than a smaller organisation and may use these to buy up the smaller organisation or force it to compete in a manner that suits the larger company;
- position: people are powerful in organisations because of the position that they hold within the organisation. Managers are more powerful than front-line staff; politicians should be more powerful than leisure officers. In addition, some less obvious positions can be considered powerful. For example, the Personal Assistant to the Chief Executive is likely to be powerful as he or she controls access to the Chief Executive. The Accounts Clerk who processes the payment of expenses will have position power, even over the Chief Executive;
- resource power: people who control access to resources within an organisation are powerful, particularly in times of resource constraint. So not only is a budget holder powerful, but the staff member who controls the allocation of staff car parks may be powerful if there is a shortage of parking facilities;
- expert power: power comes from having knowledge or abilities that are limited within an organisation. For example, the person who knows how to set up a new piece of equipment has expert power. This source of power is different from those outlined above, as it only exists for as long as there is a need for the expertise, or if no one else can develop the knowledge and skills that the expert has;
- personal power: some people are powerful in organisations simply because of who they are. It is often difficult to determine what brings about personal power, but it is likely to be linked to personal characteristics such as charisma. People with personal power will be leaders within the organisation, although they may not be managers. This is because they are able to use their personal power to motivate, influence or bring about change;
- negative power: this is the power of individuals to prevent decisions from being implemented in organisations. Much organisational decision making relies on the goodwill of staff to follow decisions and to work within the organisation's guidelines. Staff can, however, exert power over managers or the organisation by refusing to do what is being asked.

(Hersey *et al.*, 1996; Lawton and Rose, 1994; Rees and Porter, 2001)

Having considered the above sources of power, it would appear that power within local authorities should be based on organisational position, as public professionals are ultimately constrained by the position power given to members by the political process. However, the power of politicians within sport and leisure services is often not as great as expected. Policy changes, as outlined in Chapter 2, have increased the complexity and amount of decision making required of politicians involved with these services. This has led to an increasing reliance upon the information and advice offered by professionals (Nichols, 1996; Robinson, 1999a) in order to deal with the growing number of the issues that affect sport and leisure services. This expert power, which comes about because of industry-specific knowledge, makes professionals increasingly powerful within the delivery of their services.

Politics

Politics impact on the management of public sport and leisure services in two ways. First, as discussed in the previous chapter, local authorities are political organisations. Local political interests will affect the objectives to be achieved by sport and leisure, may influence investment decisions and determine the type of services to be delivered. For example, if a political party is committed to increasing access to facilities, managers may be ordered to reduce entry prices, even if this goes against good management practice.

Less obvious, but more significant, is the impact that the internal political workings have upon management. Organisational politics are difficult to describe, primarily because, like culture, it is often hard to see the politics of an organisation. In an attempt to define organisational politics, Senior (1997: p. 148) explained that politics occurs 'whenever people get together in groups and where an individual or group seeks to influence the thoughts, attitudes or behaviours of another individual or group'. This means that politics does not occur when individuals are on their own; others must be present for the politics of an organisation to be viewed. Politics is the manifestation of power.

Organisational politics have both benefits and weaknesses for the organisation. The politics of an organisation assist with team building, ensure communication and co-ordination and help to provide a framework for decision making. Conversely, politics may lead to a misuse of resources, create conflict and distract attention from the objectives of the organisation. Despite these quite serious weaknesses, all organisations have an internal political system. Politics will determine who makes the decisions in an organisation, who controls the resources, who decides what will be discussed and how conflict is resolved. Thus, in order to be effective within the organisation, public sport and leisure managers need to be aware of the politics of the organisation.

Summary and conclusions

This chapter has considered the roles and functions of management in the public sport and leisure sector. It discussed the need for managers to have general management skills, outlined desirable personality characteristics and highlighted the desirability of functional management skills. The main set of skills, however, relate to industry knowledge. The ability to provide advice and guidance on public sport and leisure and to be able to respond to the wide range of factors that impact on the delivery of services is the key to successful management.

Without knowledge of the way that services can be delivered, of the impact of legislation and the expectations and desires of customers, managers will have little opportunity to shape the direction of their services. The opportunity to shape that direction is enhanced by an understanding of the culture of the service and by the use of organisational politics to exert expert, positional and personal power.

The following section of the book is divided into six chapters that consider, in detail, the main functions required in the management of public sport and leisure services. Each chapter considers a different management function and presents the key issues and best practice in relation to the function under consideration. In addition, each chapter will discuss the implications of the public context for the function. Case study material will be provided to highlight key points and further reading and tasks for further study will be provided.

Further reading

Torkildsen, G. (1999) *Leisure and Recreation Management*, 4th edn, London: E&FN Spon.

Part II

The management of public sport and leisure services

4 Planning and strategy development

The process of planning leads to the development of organisational actions, known as strategies. Planning is the process of deciding what is to be achieved – the objectives – and how it is to be achieved – the strategy. Strategic planning emerged within the UK in the 1970s as managers struggled to find ways of coping with the growing complexity of their organisations' operating environments and the speed with which these environments were changing. Emerging initially in the commercial sector, strategic planning was advocated as the way forward for managers who wanted to take a rational and proactive approach to the direction and activities of their organisations.

This chapter discusses the planning and strategy development process that takes place within public sport and leisure services. It outlines the process of strategic planning and highlights the techniques associated with the concept. It describes the strategy process in local authorities as a whole, then focuses on the process of service review within sport and leisure services.

The process of planning

The value of planning to organisations is apparent when its benefits are considered. First, planning will result in a strategy that guides the operations of the organisation. This will provide a framework for decision making, as it will identify priorities for the organisation. The setting of objectives will force managers to ask and answer important questions, such as asking what the future opportunities are for the organisation and how targets can be set for future performance. The process of environmental auditing will make managers aware of key issues, internal strengths and weaknesses and external opportunities and threats. Finally, a strategy will help clarify staff roles, allow the allocation of resources and encourage consultation with staff.

Traditionally, strategic planning is made up of a series of activities, which have been described by Rose and Lawton, (1999: p. 123) as being 'based on a comprehensive, rational and linear approach to objective setting, implementation and appraisal, proceeding in a logical manner'. The classical strategic planning approach, advocated by Argenti (1980) is made up of five processes, which are outlined in Table 4.1.

Target setting

Corporate objectives guide the operations of the organisation as they determine what has to be delivered. Therefore it is important that these objectives are clear and communicated to and understood by everyone working within the organisation. In order to be of value in developing a strategy, objectives need to be expressed in terms that can be remembered by the acronym SMART – specific, measurable, attainable, realistic and time-constrained. Once an objective has been set, targets can be associated with these to help to focus the ensuing strategy. For example, a targeted objective could be *to provide access to green space, to 20 per cent of the community, within 2 years*. This provides a clear goal and a target for the development of plans.

Gap analysis

With these targeted objectives in mind, managers then need to evaluate the success of current plans in obtaining these objectives. This allows managers to identify changes that may need to be made to the existing strategy. For example, resources may need to be diverted from other areas in order to purchase land to provide more green space.

Table 4.1 A classical approach to strategic planning

Process	Action
Target setting	Clarify corporate objectives Set targets for objectives
Gap analysis	Forecast future performance on current strategies Identify gaps between forecasts and targets
Strategic appraisal	External appraisal Internal appraisal Identify competitive advantage Refine targets as a result of appraisal Obtain information for service plans
Strategy formulation	Generate strategic options Evaluate strategic options
Strategy implementation	Draw up action plans and budgets Monitor and control

Source: Argenti, 1980.

Strategic appraisal

This is the process of gathering information about the operating contexts, competitors and the organisation itself, in order to evaluate more fully the appropriateness of the targeted objectives. This information then informs the development of new or amended strategies and plans. The environmental appraisal process is discussed in greater detail below.

Strategy implementation

Once the strategic options have been evaluated and chosen, the plans to meet the objectives need to be incorporated into the organisation's strategy. It is likely that the service strategies of a number of departments and/or external contractors responsible for delivering services (e.g. catering or cleaning) will be interlinked and are thus affected by any changes, so it is important that the plans are carefully monitored and controlled to ensure success.

The key weakness of the classical approach to strategic planning is that it does not necessarily promote consultation with customers. This makes it possible for organisations to develop objectives that do not meet the needs and expectations of customers. In addition, the planning process itself has weaknesses. The strategy that is developed will only be as good as the information used to produce it. Managers therefore have to first, be able to gather up-to-date, relevant information and second, know how to use it. Planning is a complex task that requires skills that the organisation may not have. More importantly, however, planning is about the future and it will not get the organisation out of a current crisis.

Strategy development in local authorities

As a result of the Conservative policies of the 1980s (see Chapter 2), strategic planning began to be used by local authorities in the mid- to late 1980s. However, the use of strategic management techniques was somewhat haphazard, with many authorities claiming to have introduced strategic planning when they had done little more than simple budgeting. Recently, however, the Best Value legislation, outlined in Chapter 2, has driven strategy development within the public sector. Local authorities have been required to adopt a formal planning process in order to develop strategic plans to guide the management of the authority.

This planning process is divided into three main parts. First, local authorities have to set corporate aims and objectives. They are then required to carry out a series of fundamental performance reviews (FPRs), which result in targets being set for local authority services. Finally, local performance plans (LPPs) must be drawn up to achieve these targets and published in order to encourage accountability to the general public.

Setting corporate objectives

The corporate review process requires local authorities to develop organisational objectives, identify priorities and be clear about the values underlying these. It is important that this process involves consultation with local communities, as local authorities are accountable to the community for the services they deliver. Without consultation there is a chance that the objectives set for the authority will not reflect the needs and expectations of its citizens. This process also provides the framework for the fundamental performance reviews that follow and therefore clear and agreed organisational objectives are essential.

The Local Government Association (Sanderson, 1998) has proposed that the corporate review process should contain the following elements:

- setting and reviewing corporate objectives;
- decision making informed by community consultation as well as local political priorities;
- consideration of future issues, such as changes in legislation;
- the establishment of a corporate planning process which co-ordinates other plans and the budgetary cycle;
- co-ordination with other statutory and corporate planning processes;
- the process to inform the selection of services for fundamental performance reviews.

From this, it is apparent that the corporate objectives need to drive the planning process in a manner similar to that promoted by the classical model of strategic planning. Research carried out with local authorities that piloted Best Value found that 'the performance of Leisure Services needs to be evaluated with reference to how they contribute to the corporate aims as without this it is not possible to say how well leisure is contributing to corporate objectives' (Nichols and Robinson, 2000: p. 32). Therefore the importance of the corporate review process cannot be overstated.

Fundamental performance reviews (FPRs)

Fundamental performance reviews are required for all local authority services and a key function of the corporate planning process is to determine the criteria for selecting service priorities for performance review. Some authorities have chosen to carry out these reviews on a service-by-service basis (e.g. leisure or housing), while others have combined a number of services in a package that delivers one of the corporate objectives. For example, if a local authority wanted to review the services that contribute to its objectives for youth, it could review parts of education, leisure and health. How the services are reviewed is not overly important; what is important is that FPRs must result in the establishment of performance targets for the service or services and in the development of a clear plan that achieves these targets.

The format of FPRs is left to the local authority; however, the Best Value legislation requires authorities to:

- consider whether it should be providing the service;
- consider the level and the way in which it should be providing the service;
- consider its objectives in relation to the service;
- assess its performance in delivering the service by reference to appropriate performance indicators;
- assess the competitiveness of its performance in delivering the service by making comparisons with organisations delivering similar services;
- consult with other organisations about the delivery of the service;
- assess its success in meeting relevant performance standards or targets, or assess progress towards meeting these.

(Sanderson, 1998)

The actual process of carrying out reviews is also left up to the local authority; however, the Office of the Deputy Prime Minister (2001) has advised that fundamental performance reviews need to:

- take a long-term perspective in order to anticipate and forecast future needs and wants;
- involve elected members as these are the representatives of the community;
- seek advice from outside the authority in order to generate new ideas or to test ideas;
- involve those currently delivering the service as they have first-hand knowledge about the service;
- question existing commitments in order to challenge the methods of delivery;
- engage users and potential users of services;
- address equity considerations, as this is a key issue for local authorities.

This will ensure that the review process is comprehensive, coherent and includes all possible stakeholders. The targets and plans generated from this process are then published in local performance plans.

Local performance plans (LPPs)

Local performance plans have been described by Sanderson (1998, p. 7) as 'the main instruments by which Best Value authorities will be held accountable for delivering Best Value by their local communities'. Local performance plans will allow citizens to determine whether their views have been incorporated into local authority strategy and how the local authority is performing.

The plans report on local authority performance, making comparisons with the performance of other authorities, other organisations and against targets set in consultation with the local community. In addition, the plans must identify future objectives and targets, so that the general public can be aware of the long-term intentions of the local authority. Finally, the LPPs must outline how objectives are to be met, highlight plans for improvement, investment and expenditure and set out a means for responding to the plan.

The Office of the Deputy Prime Minister (2001) has outlined how local performance plans should include:

- a summary of the authority's objectives in respect of its functions that have been developed from the corporate vision and strategy;
- a summary of current performance;
- a comparison with performance in previous financial years in order to provide a context for current performance;
- a summary of the authority's approach to efficiency improvement, highlighting how the authority has become more efficient;
- a statement describing the review programme;
- the key results of completed FPRs including the results of consultation, the alternatives considered and the plan of action from the review;
- the performance targets set for future years;
- a plan of action which sets out targets and a means of achieving these;
- a response to audit and inspection reports, highlighting how recommendations have been acted upon;
- a consultation statement commenting on the forms, types and amount of consultation carried out in the authority;
- a financial statement.

Performance plans are then subject to audit by external assessors.

Auditing

The Audit Commission evaluates public services in order to see whether they are delivering services that meet their objectives and are working within the Best Value framework. If the Audit Commission considers the service to be 'failing', it can recommend a number of actions to the Secretary of State. The powers of the Secretary of State range from requiring an authority to increase the targets associated with a performance indicator, to major action such as removing responsibility for a function from an authority. This is a significant difference from the commercial sector, where the only audits carried out are on financial accounts. As a result of this auditing process, the Audit Commission (2002) identified seven pitfalls that public sport and leisure providers have made in the development of strategic plans. Weaknesses have been caused by:

- a lack of political guidance on corporate policy and service planning, which can result in strategies that do not reflect corporate objectives and priorities;
- unclear corporate priorities and objectives which make it difficult for service providers to identify their own priorities and objectives;
- a lack of clarity about the services that the authority will prioritise and deliver;
- a narrow strategic scope that does not reflect the diversity of local leisure interests and the range of providers in the area. This results in unco-ordinated provision and duplication of services;
- a lack of accurate information on who does and does not use the service, or on community needs;
- absence of clear solutions to strategic issues or lack of priority actions;
- language that is too complex or includes too much jargon.

Many of these pitfalls can be avoided by adopting the strategy development process outlined in Figure 2.2, supported by the environmental auditing techniques presented below.

Fundamental performance reviews in public sport and leisure

Once the corporate objectives have been set for the local authority, the process of planning and strategy development can get under way within the public sport and leisure service. Unlike the strategic planning process presented in Table 4.1, the process of FPR is not necessarily hierarchical. Providers are expected to consult at all stages of the review process and to make external comparisons. In addition, if the service does not meet required standards, management of the service can be removed from local authority control. Although the process of strategy development and planning in public sport and leisure services differs in some ways from the approach presented by Argenti (1980), the classical approach to strategic planning offers managers a number of tools to assist with their planning process. One essential tool, environmental auditing, is discussed below.

Environmental appraisal

The key to the development of a good strategy is information and awareness of the operating environments that affect the organisation. All organisations exist and operate within an external environment that determines their success, offers opportunities, presents threats and shapes strategy.

The main factors in the external environment that are of importance to organisations are customers and competitors and without an awareness of these, the organisation is unlikely to survive.

The public sector is no different from other organisations in this respect and, as a result, it is essential that managers carry out an appraisal of the external environment within which the service operates, including a competitor analysis. In addition, it is important that managers are aware of the capability of the internal environment – the service itself. This will allow managers to identify strengths of the service, such as staff, or weaknesses, such as ageing facilities.

The purpose of carrying out this analysis is to gather information that will inform strategy development. McDonald (1999) has argued that the process of internal and external assessment allows an organisation to develop an understanding of its position, within its particular market. The information gathered will also inform managers about the characteristics of their customers and competitors. In addition, managers will be aware of strengths that can be used to take advantage of opportunities and weaknesses that need protection from external threats. The process of environmental auditing ensures that the strategies developed from the FPR are fully informed, externally focused and that they build upon existing service strengths.

There are two main factors that affect the success of the environmental auditing process. First, the accuracy of the audit and the subsequent plan will only be as good as the information upon which the audit is based. It is therefore important that managers are able to access up-to-date and relevant information on trends and changes in both the internal and the external environment. Obtaining information on the internal environment should be relatively straightforward, as internal data should be readily accessible via the performance management frameworks to be discussed in Chapter 7. The external environment is more complex and managers will need to identify sources of information to inform them about this. The key point is that information needs to be actively sought; managers cannot assume that they know what is occurring in their environments.

Second, the success of environmental analysis relies on managers taking a structured approach to the review. This will ensure that all key aspects of the environment are addressed in a comprehensive manner. The danger is that without a structured approach, important changes in the environments may be missed. This is particularly important when auditing the external environment, given its size and the number of features to be considered. A commonly used structure for carrying out this analysis is the STEPV structure, which is presented below.

STEPV

Sloman and Sutcliffe (1998) have argued that it should be normal for organisations to identify with the dimensions that impact on the business environment in which they operate. Analysis of these dimensions is referred to by the acronym STEPV, which stands for the sociological, technological, economic, political and values dimensions of the external environment. By conducting such an analysis, managers can audit the business environment, identify trends and thereby effectively carry out the process of fundamental performance review.

The STEPV analysis identifies both microeconomic and macroeconomic issues. The microeconomic issues are factors that are specific to the local business market in which the organisation operates, whereas issues that affect the organisation at a national level determine the macroeconomic environment. The STEPV analysis is a critical process in the development of an organisation's strategy because it will reveal factors that will have the capacity to determine the success or failure of the strategy:

- *social* factors will be demographic features such as an ageing population, smaller households, increasing single-person households and changing lifestyles;
- *technological* factors are those that relate to advances in technology, engineering or technical skills, such as e-commerce, drug testing or equipment improvements;
- *economic* factors are features like the strength of the economy, unemployment levels, interest rates, the growing divide between those with money and those without;
- *political* factors include legislation and the political values expressed by both central and local government. Changes in employment legislation are political factors, as is the Labour Party's Social Inclusion Agenda;
- *values* are those things that customers consider to be important, which often guide their buying decisions and choice of service provider. For example, in the early 1990s, at the height of the 'green movement', customers valued organisations and services that were considered to be environmentally sound.

A STEPV analysis for a sport and leisure centre is outlined in Table 4.2.

Internal audits

Johnson and Scholes (1999) have proposed that the auditing of the internal environment should focus on four basic areas:

- physical resources: the actual items at the disposal of the service, such as equipment or facilities, the age and condition of these items and the potential to use these items to enhance or gain competitive advantage;

Table 4.2 Examples of STEPV factors affecting a public sport and leisure centre

Sociological	Increasing population aged over 40 Increasing car ownership Increasing age of couples having children, which has led to greater discretionary income among 18–24 year olds Increase in shift working, which decreases 'off-peak' periods
Technological	Improvements in equipment manufacturing leading to longer-lasting equipment, needing less maintenance Advances in management information systems allowing more informed managerial decision making
Economic	Increasing interest of the commercial sector who have financial resources Greater discretionary income amongst those who have money An increasing percentage of the population that does not have money
Political	Best Value legislation Political leadership of the authority Minimum wage legislation Working hours directive (prevents long shifts) Health and Safety legislation
Values	Customers value high-quality services and make choices based on value for money Child protection concerns

- human resources: the service's staff in terms of the roles required, the skills and experience available and the ability of staff to adapt to potential changes;
- financial resources: how the organisation is financed and funded, the management of income and expenditure and the relationship with key financial stakeholders, such as Sport England, commercial partners or banks;
- operational resources: such as how the service operates, where it operates, the resources required by different services and how the services are perceived.

Within these areas managers need to examine and evaluate past performance. The purpose of this is to try to account for why the service has had its past successes and failures. It is not enough to just be aware of the success and/or failure of service strategies; managers must be able to explain or account for these in order to learn from the past. Next the manager must evaluate current practices within the organisation. There are a number of approaches for doing this evaluation; however, the Quest framework outlined in Chapter 8 is appropriate for this activity. This should focus on what is actually happening, not what policies or strategic documents say should happen. This will ensure that the audit actually reflects the existing internal environment.

SWOT analysis

It is important to note that these techniques do not tell the manager what to do; they are simply techniques for arranging information in order to make sense of complex environments. The information from these audits assists with the completion of the four Cs approach to the fundamental performance review. Auditing will provide managers with contextual information, lead to an increased awareness of resources, identify stakeholders and priorities for the review and thus underpin the FPR process.

Table 4.3 shows what one team of managers and staff came up with, after carrying out an audit using the SWOT approach.

Table 4.3 SWOT Analysis for Belper Leisure Centre Trust

Strengths	*Weaknesses*
Trust status allows independent approach	Low level of professional training
Stakeholder support	Lack of fitness suite
Flexible staff	Access in and around the Centre
Location in area	Location of catering facility
Financial independence	Blame culture prevalent among staff
Customer support/loyalty	Lack of team work
Fiscal advantages – business rates	Bar facilities
VAT	Lack of progressive investment
Income surplus retention	Lack of an 'all weather' facility
Growing local customer base	Lack of a crèche
Lifeguard training	Energy conservation is poor
Health and safety	Age of Centre
Car parking facilities	Poor visibility from the road
Room for expansion	Old plant and equipment
Advertising strategy	Costs of removal of hazardous materials
Image of Centre	Agendas of some Trustees and partners
Current lack of major competitors	
Excellent transport links	
Opportunities	*Threats*
Capital investment programme	Changes in Health and Safety legislation
Increasing awareness of the benefits of exercise	Increasing culture of litigation
Lifestyle changes towards improving health	Increasing competition
Corporate customers	
Consultation with customers	
Benchmarking against competitors	
Use of PIs to improve management	
Investors in People Award	
Increased market share of leisure	
Branded image of service	
Lottery funding	
Increasing number of professionals living in area	

Source: Belper Leisure Centre Trust Business Plan, 2002.

The following section looks at how the four Cs should be approached in public sport and leisure services.

Challenging the role of public sport and leisure services

The nature and provision of public services must fit within the corporate objectives and strategic plan of the local authority. Policy links with corporate objectives must be made explicit and this requires providers to move beyond asking *How can local authorities best provide sport and recreation facilities?* to asking *How can council investment best be deployed in order to meet the needs of our community?* (Audit Commission, 2002: p. 1).

The purpose of this process is to move away from the assumption that the tradition of providing facility-based activities is the best way to meet the sport and leisure needs of their communities. Providers should ask questions like:

*   how much of the local economy is devoted to sport and leisure activities?
*   how can they ensure that resources are used to best effect?
*   what are they trying to achieve with facilities and programmes?
*   who is the sport and leisure service trying to cater for and why?
*   how can sport and leisure activities in non-council settings be promoted?

The process of environmental auditing will help managers to answer these questions and will provide information to assist with the 'challenge' component of Best Value.

This questioning drives the FPR process, as the whole review is about determining the best way to deliver the service. In order to meet the requirements of the challenge component of the Best Value legislation, providers need to establish what their communities want from the service and compare this with existing services. They also need to consider alternative ways of delivering the service. Challenge therefore provides the rationale for fundamental performance review.

Consultation in public sport and leisure services

Consultation is a statutory part of the Best Value legislation and providers are required to consult fully with a range of stakeholders. It is important to note that virtually all sport and leisure providers carried out user consultation prior to Best Value; however, Nichols and Robinson (2000) found that as a result of the Best Value legislation consultative practices have been extended greatly.

Consultation needs to be widespread and carefully targeted to include all key groups affected by the service. Davies and Girdler (2000) identified how providers had spent considerable time and effort in identifying the most appropriate groups for consultation. These include the following:

- dedicated users: those who book and possibly pay for using the service, such as individuals, teams and event organisers. In addition, this includes users of free facilities such as children's play areas;
- indirect users: those who benefit from the provision of the service without actually using it, such as parents whose children use sport and leisure facilities or members of the public who receive the visual benefits of parks;
- the general public: residents, businesses, council tax payers, commuters and visitors;
- staff: those involved in the delivery of the service with a vested interest in its future.

There are a variety of methods that can be used to carry out consultation and these include:

- user forums, representing interest groups, which discuss issues of importance to the groups;
- customer satisfaction questionnaires, which ask customers how they feel about the service;
- questionnaires for specific user groups such as schools, corporate customers and clubs;
- meetings with staff to find out how customers perceive the service and their thoughts on the service;
- focus groups and workshops that consider specific issues to do with the service;
- comments systems and procedures;
- 'mystery shopper visits' by customers or other authorities;
- community or area panels made up of citizens of the authority.

Nichols and Robinson (2000) found that the results of consultation were being built into decision making. In order to ensure that consultation is effective, it is important that managers are clear about what the consultation is to achieve, what will happen as a result of the process and that the process is supported and resourced adequately.

Comparing performance of public sport and leisure services

The Best Value legislation requires service providers to compare their current and future performance against other public sector bodies, and against those in the private and voluntary sectors. As a result, comparison of sport and leisure service performance occurs in three ways (Nichols and

Robinson, 2000). First, as outlined in the discussion on internal auditing, managers compare current performance with past performance in order to identify and account for improvements or declines in performance. Second, managers have to compare the performance of their service against the national performance indicators to be discussed in Chapter 7. This enables a national picture of performance to be developed. Finally, the requirement to meet targets and to improve service quality has led to the process of benchmarking, where sport and leisure services compare themselves with other similar services in order to make evaluations about performance.

The research carried out by Nichols and Robinson (2000) highlighted two key issues to do with comparison of sport and leisure services. First, providers expressed concerns about the consistency of the information used to construct measures of performance and felt that consistent and open methods of reporting comparisons needed to be established. Second, and more importantly, Nichols and Robinson (2000) highlighted a tendency to change the object of comparison to present the best possible performance. For example, when reporting performance in the LPP, it is possible to compare at the national level for some aspects of the service and at the local level for others. It is also possible to change these levels in future years. This is clearly not desirable as it leads to an inconsistent approach to comparison.

Demonstrating competitiveness

The Best Value framework requires local authorities to demonstrate that they are delivering their services in the most effective and efficient manner. To do this, they are required to show that they can compete with other possible providers. The main way of demonstrating competitiveness has been to identify and evaluate alternative ways of delivering leisure provision.

The White Paper on Best Value (DETR, 1998a: pp. 72–73) sets out six ways in which local authorities can demonstrate competitiveness under the Best Value legislation. These are:

- by commissioning an independent report, so that the local authority can reorganise its service to match the performance of the best private and public sector providers. For example, local authorities that wish to offer health and fitness activities could learn from how commercial sector health and fitness clubs run their services;
- by providing a core in-house service and buying in additional services from an external contractor, enabling comparisons to be made with the external service and appropriate improvements introduced where necessary. Public providers could fund discounted use of a commercial sector facility, rather than providing their own health and fitness facilities;

- by contracting out the service after competition amongst external providers only;
- by forming a partnership following competition to find an external partner;
- by tendering for part of a service, with the in-house team bidding against external providers;
- by disposing of or selling off the service and its assets to another provider by competitive tender.

It is important that managers conduct a robust appraisal of the options and alternatives in order to identify the most appropriate means of service delivery. These should meet strategic goals, the needs of users and potential users, and fall within capital and revenue resources. Research carried out by the Audit Commission (2002) showed that the main four options explored by those providing sport and recreation services are:

- continuation of in-house provision: more than 300 DSOs run public sport and leisure facilities;
- externalisation or partnership with a private sector provider: the London Borough of Newham has such a partnership with Greenwich Leisure Ltd. Newham's funding of Greenwich Leisure Ltd is £400,000 less than for its DSO, which previously ran the service;
- setting up a trust: Dacorum Borough Council in Hertfordshire is planning the process of transferring its sports centres and the Sports Development Service to an industrial and provident society. It is anticipated that the transfer to trust status will achieve financial savings of approximately £400,000;
- a public/private partnership: the London Borough of Bexley operates three swimming centres that are in poor condition and need heavy investment. Since funding was not available internally, the council offered a 30-year lease in exchange for the redevelopment, financing and operation of three integrated leisure centres.

Strategies and plans

At the end of the FPR, managers should be clear about the objectives for their service, the way services should be delivered and whom the service should be targeting. The Audit Commission (2002: p. 19) have outlined how:

> By challenging traditional approaches to service delivery, by exploiting the widening choice of delivery mechanisms and providers, and by facing up to the gap between service demands and the availability of resources, authorities will be better placed to find the best way of delivering sport and recreation services that are appropriate to their local context.

The vision for Taunton Deane Cultural Services is encapsulated in the following statement:

It is a vision which strives to consolidate our cultural heritage while, at the same time, developing a vibrant and creative future, contributing to the Borough's social and economic well being and enriching all our lives.

(Taunton Deane Borough Council, 2000: p. 4)

The Cultural Plan for Taunton Deane contains the following sections:

- people: this covers rural communities, inclusion and young people;
- places: this includes urban environment for living, stewardship of our heritage and facility provision;
- programmes: this contains healthy lifestyles, lifelong learning and countryside recreation.

An example of action the local authority will take for these sections is presented below. It is important to note that each section contains a comprehensive and coherent package of actions, all aimed at ensuring that the vision of the Cultural Strategy is met. In addition, the document contains clear outcomes for each section.

Section	Action
Rural communities	Assist villages to make plans for recreational activities in their area, particularly where new housing developments may offer financial contributions for community facilities
Inclusion	Provide free access to our sports facilities for carers of disabled people
Young people	Develop a range of arts activities for the 16–21 age range aimed at maintaining their interest in the arts after leaving school
An urban environment for living	Identify opportunities to create new areas of public open space
Stewardship of our heritage	Ensure the use of good design and materials which respect and enhance local character and distinctiveness
Facility provision	Continue to develop programmes and events in and around the County Museum
Healthy lifestyles	Promote existing long-distance cycleways, bridleways and footpaths as tourist and recreational attractions
Lifelong learning	Develop and promote sports courses which give people the skills to participate in physical activities at recreational level
Countryside recreation	Publish information about opportunities for recreation in the countryside

Figure 4.1 A cultural plan for Taunton Deane, 2000–2005.

Source: Taunton Deane Borough Council, 2000.

   This information then needs to be encapsulated into a strategic plan that guides the operations of the service in order to meet its objectives. The Department of Culture, Media and Sport requires local authorities to produce a local cultural strategy, which provides the overarching framework for the management of all cultural services offered by the local authority. The cultural strategy contributes to the local authority's local performance plan and is broken down into the main components that make up Cultural Services. These components each have their own service plan, which provides the plans and direction for the service. Excerpts from the cultural strategy for Taunton Deane Borough Council are provided in Figure 4.1.

Summary and conclusions

This chapter has considered the process of planning and strategy development in public sport and leisure services. Although the planning process within these services differs slightly from that of the classical model developed by Argenti (1980), the end result is the same – the development of a strategic plan to guide the operations of the service. The public sector process is more complicated, requiring greater consultation and a challenge to their existing role, which is absent in the commercial sector model. As a result, it is possible to suggest that the public sector strategy development process outlined in this chapter is, in fact, more thorough than that followed by the commercial sector.

Suggested tasks for further study

- Carry out a STEPV analysis of a public sport and leisure service of your choice.
- Attempt to develop targeted objectives for a youth sport session.
- List all of the relevant stakeholders who should be involved in the strategy development of a public sport and leisure service of your choice.
- Identify mechanisms for carrying out this consultation.
- Obtain a copy of the cultural strategy and service plans of a public sport and leisure provider and identify how the service plan contributes to the cultural plan.

Further reading

Audit Commission (2002) *Sport and Recreation: Learning from audit, inspection and research*, London: Audit Commission.

5   Human resource management

This chapter discusses the function of human resource management (HRM) within the public sport and leisure industry. It considers briefly the emergence of the concept of human resource management and then goes on to consider the issues and procedures that are involved in the effective management of people, discussing recruitment and selection, continuing staff development, discipline and conflict. The chapter ends with a consideration of the issues involved in managing 'external workers' such as development staff.

Human resource management as a key management task

The field of human resource management (also called personnel management) has gradually evolved over the last century, increasing in sophistication until it is now considered a strategic management discipline in its own right. Its roots were founded in the widespread recognition that a specialised personnel function was needed with the growth of large organisations in the late 1800s and early 1900s, and the associated human and social problems that arose as a result.

The 1930s saw the start of the human relations movement, which was concerned with releasing human potential through effective leadership and communication. This led to an increase in technology and research in such areas as interviewing and selection as it became apparent that it was possible to ensure that the best candidate was employed for a job. As a result, personnel departments were set up, gained status and started to play a role in employment decisions, promotion and training.

The rise of unions substantially increased the status and power of personnel departments. Organisations began to rely on these departments to counter the unions' efforts to organise the company, or to deal with the union when this failed. Another major change, starting in the 1960s, resulted from the development of employment law. As a result of the increased risk of lawsuits for poor personnel practice, fair employment practices became increasingly important. Again, personnel departments gained in status, more for what they could do to protect the organisation than for any contribution they made to organisational effectiveness.

At this stage, personnel departments were seen to have a purely administrative and service function; their role was to carry out a collection of ad hoc tasks, such as maintaining personnel records, placing job advertisements, preparing employment contracts and dealing with unions. However, during the 1980s, it became increasingly apparent that the management of people was a critical management function and that staff could be viewed as the major resource of an organisation. This was particularly the case in the service sector. Fundamental changes in the business environment, such as rising costs, rapid technological changes and flatter, leaner, more flexible organisations, meant that employees, as a resource, had to be managed in a planned and co-ordinated way. Thus, those involved in human resource management became responsible for identifying and developing people with the talents and imagination that organisations needed to compete in a changing, complex and competitive world (Beer *et al.*, 1984).

Over the last decade, however, the responsibility for recruitment, development and appraisal of staff has moved away from the human resource (HR) specialists and is now the responsibility of individual managers. As a result, the work of HRM departments has returned to being primarily administrative, but has also gained a strategic responsibility for the development of employment policies. Human resource management is therefore about control and co-ordination of employee behaviour in pursuit of organisational goals, primarily through the application of employment policies.

An employment policy is a documented strategy that integrates the organisation's various personnel policies to enable it to effectively utilise its human resources to meet the changing requirements of the environment, technology and the market. Local authorities will have employment policies, which cover aspects of pay and conditions, recruitment, appraisal and promotion, health and safety and employee involvement. Although managers have to work within the guidelines set out by these policies, it is important to realise that, although such policies deal with the needs of the organisation, they do not necessarily deal with the needs of teams or individual staff. The shift of HR responsibility to individual managers is a result of the recognition that it is managers that are aware of the strengths and weakness of their staff as they work most closely with them. Thus, HRM has become part of a manager's job.

Frameworks governing HRM practice

Management of people occurs within a legal and regulatory framework, within which there are two key areas that govern and influence human resource management. The first of these areas is equal opportunities and

the second is employment law. The issues covered by these two areas of
legislation change frequently and it is important that managers have a
means of staying up to date with current legislation. Most local authorities
will have a legal department to help with this, but managers have a
responsibility to have a working knowledge of the current laws governing
equal opportunities and employment.

Equal opportunities

Equal opportunities is one area where the organisation must have documented policies, as employees cannot be discriminated against on the
grounds of gender, race, disability, belonging to a trade union or having a
'spent' conviction. In order to protect both the organisation and its
employees from discriminatory practices, it is important that public sport
and leisure providers have a clear policy on equal opportunities. An
extract from Brighton and Hove City Council's policy is shown in Figure
5.1 as an example of good practice. It is worth noting that this policy goes
beyond what is legally required, indicating a solid commitment to equal
opportunities.

All of the organisation's activities and policies should ensure equal
opportunities in the work place for all staff, avoiding both direct and indirect discriminatory practices. *Direct discrimination* occurs when one individual is treated less favourably than another, on one of the prohibited
grounds outlined above. For example, sexual harassment is direct discrimination. *Indirect discrimination* occurs when an individual is penalised by
implication; for example, rejecting a female job applicant on the basis that
she may become pregnant.

Equal opportunities is becoming increasingly important as legislation
evolves to cover customers as well. For example, the Disability Discrimination Act (1995) requires public sport and leisure providers to ensure that
people with disabilities can access the same service, at the same level of
quality, as those without disabilities. These services must therefore be
equal opportunity organisations in all aspects of their operations.

Brighton and Hove City Council is committed to Equal Opportunities in employment
and service delivery. It seeks to ensure equal opportunities for all, combating all
forms of discrimination on the basis of race, colour, ethnic or national origins, creed,
gender, sexual orientation or marital status and disability or age. This applies to
recruitment, training, pay and conditions of service for employees, design and delivery of service for customers, and strategic planning and policy formation.

Figure 5.1 Brighton and Hove City Council Equal Opportunities policy.

Source: www.brighton-hove.gov.uk

Employment law

In addition to ensuring that all HRM activities ensure equal opportunities, public sport and leisure providers also have to ensure that their management activities take place within the legal framework of employment law. Services are not only affected by UK employment law, but also by that issued from the European Union and thus the need to stay up to date with current law is imperative.

There are a number of statutory rights that employees are entitled to, which range from the right to a written statement of terms of employment, to the right not to be unfairly dismissed. Most employment rights have a qualification period, which means that a member of staff must work for an organisation for a certain period of time before they are entitled to the right. Some rights, however, have no qualification period and due to the fact that employment legislation continuously evolves, managers must identify a source of up-to-date information to ensure that they are working within the legal framework.

Tasks in the management of people

The next section looks at the key HRM functions that are carried out in a public sport and leisure service. It considers the tasks of recruitment and selection, continuing staff development and managing discipline and grievance, and highlights key issues within these important functions.

Recruitment and selection

The recruitment and selection of new staff is critical to the successful delivery of sport and leisure services. One of the factors that characterises the sport and leisure industry is the impact that the people delivering the service make on those who avail themselves of the service. Recruitment and selection is therefore the responsibility of individual managers and cannot be left up to the HRM department.

Recruitment

Recruitment is the process of attracting suitable candidates to a vacant post and is made up of two parts – job analysis and attracting candidates – which are discussed below.

JOB ANALYSIS

This is any systematic procedure for obtaining detailed and objective information about a job, task or role that will be performed, or is currently being performed. There are five key reasons for carrying out job analysis. First, it is necessary to establish the purpose of the job, in order to establish whether the post is still necessary to the organisation. Second, the possibility of redefining the post, or combining aspects of the post with other jobs, needs to be evaluated. This may make the post, or posts, more fulfilling for staff. Third, the job arrangements need to be evaluated. This means considering whether the job could be full time, part time or shared; or if it could be carried out in a facility, or in the community. Fourth, an analysis of the job will identify the tasks of the post and the outcomes and objectives the post-holder has to achieve. These can then be incorporated into a job description for the post. Finally, job analysis allows managers to identify the skills and knowledge required by the post. These can then be used to develop a person specification (see below), which should be used for selection when filling the post.

There are a number of methods available for carrying out job analysis and any combination of the following will allow managers to generate accurate information about posts in the organisation:

- interview the current jobholder about the role and the requirements of the role;
- provide the jobholder with a list of tasks and ask them to indicate which apply to the job;
- ask the jobholder to keep a diary of what they do;
- observe the jobholder to see what they do;
- ask others what they feel the job entails;
- do the job for a few days to see what it entails.

(Cook, 1998)

It is important that this process is carried out to ensure that the documentation used to guide recruitment and selection – the job description and person specification – is appropriate and relevant to the post.

A *job description* is a statement of the component tasks, duties, objectives, standards and environmental circumstances of a job and is a legal requirement for all posts. It is, however, often one of the least useful documents in the recruitment and selection process, as job descriptions are rarely updated, leading to the recruitment of inappropriate staff. It is therefore essential that the job description accurately reflects the tasks that the employee is expected to carry out and should be drawn up from the analysis of the job. Figure 5.2 shows the job description of a Project Manager for Sheffield City Council.

The *person specification* is sometimes called a job specification. This document is based on the job description and describes the type of person required to do the job (Figure 5.3). This includes:

- qualifications: this should highlight qualifications that are relevant to the post, such as first aid qualifications, coaching certificates or management training;

Sheffield
City Council

City of Sheffield
JOB DESCRIPTION

DEPARTMENT	DEVELOPMENT, ENVIRONMENT AND LEISURE
DIVISION/SECTION	LEISURE SERVICES – SPORT AND COMMUNITY RECREATION
POST TITLE	Slice Card Project Manager
	18.5 hours per week
RESPONSIBLE TO	CLIENT AND PARTNERSHIP MANAGER
RESPONSIBLE FOR	Staff, volunteers and secondees as appropriate
HOLIDAY AND	Cover for/by Client and Partnership Manager
SICKNESS RELIEF	Cover for/by other officers within the Client and Partnership team
PURPOSE OF JOB	To manage the City Council's Slice Card Scheme. This is a discount card for leisure, available to certain priority groups. To work under the direction of the Client and Partnership Manager to deliver agreed service targets for the designated areas of responsibility.

SPECIFIC DUTIES AND RESPONSIBILITIES   **Slice Card Manager**

- To manage the Slice Card Project within the Client and Partnership Team having due regard to the Council's fundamental policy commitments to effective client service provision and promotion of equal opportunities, a health and safety culture and good employee relations.
- To implement policies, plans and budgets and deliver effective services within legislative requirements and City Council policies.
- To develop and manage effective partnerships with agencies who can sell, distribute or promote the Slice Card on behalf of the Council.
- To develop effective and customer focused procedures for the sale of the card to the key target groups.
- To assist the Client and Partnership Manager in the development of Slice Card pricing policies, and to monitor pricing to ensure compliance with Slice discounts.
- To liaise with the relevant agencies to ensure that criteria for eligibility are kept up to date to ensure the card reaches appropriate groups.
- To manage the design and purchase of cards, promotional and point-of-sale information and to ensure effective distribution to all sales outlets.
- To co-ordinate and deliver sales training to front-line staff in all partner agencies.
- To contribute to the section's service plan.
- To develop and implement promotional plans to maximise card sales.
- To develop budgetary plans for the operation of the scheme in conjunction with the Client and Partnership Manager.
- To maintain effective systems to monitor and evaluate the effectiveness of the scheme and to commission appropriate research.
- To keep abreast of developments in the public sport and leisure sector in respect of leisure card schemes for disadvantaged groups.
- To develop opportunities for external funding or sponsorship to support the card scheme.
- To contribute to continuous improvement through the use of the Quest Quality Scheme for Leisure.
- To be responsible for safe working practices as defined by Directorate and City Council Policy ensuring the development, monitoring and maintenance of safe systems of work.
- Any other duties as may arise.
- All duties and responsibilities should be carried out within agreed Council policies and procedures, in particular the Council's policy on equal opportunities and health and safety.

Figure 5.2 Example of a job description.

Source: Reproduced by courtesy of Sheffield City Council.

Table 5.1 Methods of external recruitment

Method	Strengths	Weaknesses
School/university 'milk rounds'	Can deal with large numbers in one visit	Limited to lower level positions Can be costly and time-consuming
Newspaper advertisements	Wide distribution, easily accessible, can be done immediately	Expensive, not necessarily targeted to appropriate candidates
Advertisements in professional journals	Goes to target group	May take time before publication, costly
Internet advertising	Cheap, immediately available	Not necessarily targeted, only accessible to computer users
Recruitment from job centres	Cheap, candidates live locally	Limited supply of candidates
Recruitment agencies	Wide network of contacts, someone else does all the work	Very expensive and useful only for senior management

Source: Adapted from Thomson, 1997.

It may not be possible to include all of this information in a small advertisement and if this is the case, the key points to include are the essential features of the person specification and a point of contact.

Applications

Most public sport and leisure services ask applicants to complete an application form when applying for vacant posts. All application forms need to be adapted to the advertised post and should be designed to obtain the maximum information possible about the applicant that is relevant to the requirements of the job. It therefore needs to be based on the person specification. The application form should provide all of the information required to shortlist applicants to become candidates for the offered post.

It is important that the information required by the application form is relevant. Public sport and leisure services rarely update their application forms, which may require information on marital status, number of children, religion or ethnic background. Not only is this information irrelevant for most positions, but it can also lead to discrimination in the shortlisting process. If it is to be included on application forms, those responsible for recruitment have to be certain that such information does not affect their judgement of the applicant, which should be on the essential characteristics alone.

Selection

Selection is the process by which the post-holder is chosen from the applicants and selection methods must be fair and designed as much as possible to predict a candidate's future performance in the job. The purpose of selection is to generate information about the candidate in order to enable comparisons with other candidates and thus assist decision making. It is therefore important that organisations do not rely solely on one method of selection, as a single selection method is unlikely to provide all of the information required to make an accurate decision. Therefore a combination of the methods, as outlined in Table 5.2, should be used when making the decision about who to appoint.

Selection begins with the shortlisting of applicants, which, as mentioned earlier, must be done on the basis of the essential characteristics required to do the job. This will usually lead to applicants being rejected and it is both morally and practically right to let them know that first, they have been rejected and second, why. This will enable the applicant to learn from the experience.

Having decided which candidates are to take part in the selection process, it is then necessary to inform the candidates of when, where and how the selection will be made. Selection should be made on information about the candidate's ability to meet the essential characteristics of the job and the methods utilised should allow this information to be generated. For example, if the post is for a lifeguard, they may be required to demonstrate that they can swim, as this can be considered an essential characteristic.

The most commonly used technique for selecting who to hire is the selection interview. Although the interview has been challenged on the grounds of validity, for many organisations it is the only way that managers have of finding out adequate information about the applicants and of providing applicants with enough information in order to make a decision about taking the job.

There are a number of ways that the interview can be made more reliable. First, the interview must be structured, with the questions asked in the interview being based on the person specification and job description as they must be relevant to the job. Second, interviewers must have a list of questions or a checklist to ensure that they ask all candidates the same information and that they get all of the information required. Third, more than one person should carry out the interview in order to avoid personal bias. Fourth, there must be a clear, valid and consistent method of scoring candidates and finally, interviewers must be trained in interview techniques and equal opportunities.

Once a selection decision has been made, the successful candidate should be offered the job as soon as is appropriate. The contract of employment and other paperwork should then be sent to the appointed person in order to complete the recruitment and selection process.

Table 5.2 Methods of selection

Method	Strengths	Weaknesses
Application forms	Cheap Easy to administer Provides information to assist with initial selection decision Information can be verified	Information is not detailed enough
Psychometric tests (Tests of ability and personality)	Can test verbal and mental skills Can establish personality characteristics	Need to be administered by trained personnel Often unreliable Can be discriminatory
In-tray prioritisation exercises (Candidates are asked to deal with a series of memos, reports and tasks)	Shows ability to identify priorities in the tasks to be completed Shows ability of candidate to deal with written material Shows time-management skills	May not be 'real' and therefore are not good predictors of behaviour Require candidates to have had experience of the type of job they are applying for
Work samples (Candidates are asked to bring in examples of work or projects that they have completed in the past)	Indicates the ability to complete projects May provide evidence of experience and the ability to perform tasks required of the advertised post	Difficult to verify as candidates' own work
Assessment centres	Evaluation can be done by a number of people, using a variety of tasks and a number of exercises Are a valid and reliable process of selection	Time-consuming and expensive
References	Provide an alternative impression of the candidate Allows key details to be checked Provides an assessment of the candidates' work performance	Can be biased Are increasingly becoming of little value as companies provide the minimum of information in order to avoid litigation
Interviews	Allow face-to-face contact with candidates Allow additional details to be obtained Allow the candidates to ask questions Are flexible	Not particularly reliable as a method of selection Can lead to discrimination and bias

Continuing staff development

Continuing staff development is a process that ensures that staff are performing to the best of their ability and are able to take advantage of career development opportunities within the organisation. The staff development process should start from the day a recruit joins the organisation and will finish with an exit interview when they leave, and it is important to realise that there will be times where people have to leave the organisation in order to progress in their career. The major components of the development process are outlined below.

Induction

When a new employee starts work it is essential that they are inducted into the job and the organisation by a carefully prepared induction programme. An induction programme aims to familiarise the new employee with the organisation, health and safety matters, general conditions of employment and the work of the department in which they are employed. It aims to integrate the new employee into the culture of the organisation and to make them effective in their post as soon as possible.

A good induction programme has benefits for both staff and the organisation. First of all, the costs of recruitment are reduced, as employees are given a fair chance to master the work and are less likely to leave or to make mistakes. Induction will reduce the stress of starting a new job and allow the new recruit to feel part of the team. It will also establish any immediate training needs. Finally, there is a legal requirement to inform staff of the health and safety laws affecting their jobs and this provides the ideal opportunity to do this.

An induction programme should be arranged for all new appointments, whether internal or external and at whatever level of the organisation. It should begin before the person starts work by sending out details of the organisation and any handbook that exists. The programme should be designed in consultation with the new recruit. The information that should be covered in an induction programme is outlined below and the organisation of information must take into account the attention span of the individual, the complexity of the information and the priority of information. It is helpful to use an induction checklist to ensure that all necessary information has been given.

Induction programmes must cover:

- any training requirements needed to do the job;
- health and safety requirements;
- information about the organisation, although this could have been sent prior to the candidate starting;
- documentation necessary to begin work, such as bank details, P60, car parking pass, identity cards;

- working arrangements, such as hours of work, break times, policy on working at home, lieu time;
- remuneration arrangements, such as when and how staff are paid, increases in salary and pensions;
- holiday arrangements, such as when leave can be taken and how to book it;
- site facilities, such as fitness facilities, cafeterias, car parking.

The new recruit should complete a meaningful task as soon as possible so that they get an idea of what will be required of them and the standard at which they have to perform. In addition, to help the new member of staff to be integrated into the organisation, it is good practice to allocate a 'buddy' to assist them with their induction. If induction arrangements are successful, the new recruit will have been allowed a fair chance to master the work required and will quickly be performing at a high standard.

Performance appraisal

Once an individual has become part of an organisation, the organisation's appraisal process will then guide their continuing development. The key function of performance appraisal is to provide the opportunity for feedback to be given to staff regarding their performance. It is often the only time formally set aside to investigate current performance and individual strengths and weaknesses. Critten (1994) has argued that the principles that underlie performance appraisal are first, a need for clear standards of performance for every member of staff and second, a culture which encourages clear communication and sharing of such standards and feedback to individuals following any appraisal or evaluation.

Performance appraisal systems are important for setting objectives and establishing levels of performance. The appraisal should be concerned predominantly with improving current performance, rather than assessing past performance. Appraisal systems should also allow training needs to be identified. Poole and Warner (1998) and Rees and Porter (2001) have suggested that an appraisal system should have some of the following purposes:

- auditing of individuals and departments to discover their work potential;
- discovering training needs;
- succession planning to identify potential for promotion or other roles;
- motivation of staff to reach organisational standards and objectives;
- developing staff by offering advice, praise, sanctions and information;
- improving standards and thus performance.

Performance appraisal is an important part of the staff development process and as Slack (1997) has highlighted, there are some key issues that need to be considered in order to ensure that an organisation's performance management system is as effective as possible. First, appraisals must be relevant in that the objectives set and the criteria used for evaluation must be directly relevant to the job and the jobholder. For example, a lifeguard cannot be assessed against revenue targets, as someone in this position is unlikely to have the level of authority to affect costs and revenue. Second, the method used to evaluate performance must be reliable, so that everyone who is responsible for assessing job performance evaluates performance in the same way. Finally, the appraisal system must be supported by the organisation – it must be resourced adequately, decisions made at appraisal must be followed through and senior management must be committed to it.

If these issues are addressed, the performance appraisal process will underpin the staff development process. It is important to note, however, that assessment of performance should not be a formal once-a-year undertaking, but should be a continuous process throughout the year. Although many organisations have set appraisal periods, employees should receive continuous, objective and constructive feedback about their performance in order to develop fully.

Training

Poole and Warner (1998: p. 643) have described training as:

> any systematic process used by organisations to develop employees' knowledge, skills, behaviours, or attitudes in order to contribute to the achievement of the organisation's goals.

Also referred to as human resource development, once people have been recruited, job training is a key factor in ensuring that they do their jobs well. Many organisations consider training to be expensive (particularly if people are going to leave); however, the benefits of training far outweigh the costs and training should be regarded as an investment in the human capital of the organisation.

Critten (1994) has argued that training needs to be viewed as a process of learning that leads to behaviour change, rather than a series of events and courses. He argues that, in order for training to be of value to the organisation, it must be tailored to individual needs and delivered in a way that meets individual learning styles (Honey and Mumford, 1992). Figure 5.4 outlines the process to be followed in ensuring that training is effective within public sport and leisure services.

Training needs analysis is a way of establishing the training needs of an individual and should be carried out when staff first start work, with job or technology changes and when there is a change in priorities for organisation. It is important to carry this out as it ensures that training

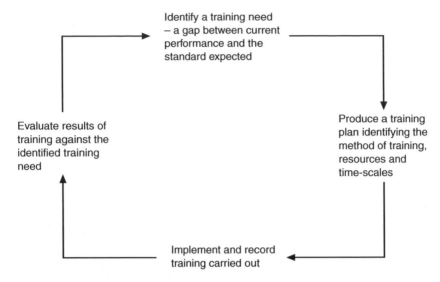

Figure 5.4 The four-stage cycle of systemic training.
Source: Adapted from Critten, 1994.

contributes to the achievements of the organisation's goals (Poole and Warner, 1998). It is usual to identify training needs during an appraisal interview or at the start of an induction programme. Training needs analysis is carried out following the steps outlined below:

- break up activities required of the job into a series of tasks;
- describe the knowledge and skills required to perform each task;
- assess the jobholder against the identified knowledge and skills;
- discuss with the jobholder their perceived requirements;
- consider personal development needs.

From this analysis a *training plan* can be developed, clarifying training objectives and identify training methods. The training plan can then be carried out and evaluated against the established objectives. This is of key importance to ensure that staff have actually learned what is required: without this evaluation, the effectiveness of training cannot be assessed. The success of training should be demonstrated by improvements in performance, which should be noted at the next performance appraisal. At this stage, further training or development needs will be identified and the process of staff development continues.

Discipline and grievance procedures

Maintaining discipline among staff is a key managerial skill and can be made more effective by the techniques outlined in Chapter 3. There are, however, times when the severity of performance or action requires a formal procedure to bring about change and this procedure is called a disciplinary procedure. In addition, there may be times when staff feel that the behaviour of others in the organisation is unacceptable and wish to express this formally. This is done through the grievance procedure.

Grievances

A grievance is an expression of dissatisfaction by an individual or group in respect to any aspect of their working conditions. Thomson (1997) outlines how a grievance usually starts with some sort of trigger, usually in the form of management action (such as changes in shifts), which gives rise to dissatisfaction. At the early stages dissatisfaction can be dealt with informally; however, if it is ignored or handled badly, it is likely to become a more formalised and serious grievance.

Bouwen and Salipante (1990) have identified four distinct stages through which a grievance can pass. The first of these is the *private formulation* of a grievance when individuals start to feel dissatisfied or feel unfairly treated, but keep these feelings to themselves. The second stage occurs when they begin to talk about their dissatisfaction – this is the *public formulation* stage. At this stage the individual is looking for help and support and may try to achieve this by distorting what actually occurred. The third stage identified by Bouwen and Salipante (1990) is the stage of *action*, which may involve a formal or informal statement of grievance to people in authority or a decrease in productivity or overtime work. Finally, there is the *outcome* stage when the grievance is settled or the individual leaves the organisation.

Handling grievances takes diplomacy, trust and openness; however, there are also legal requirements that have to be adhered to. All organisations must provide employees with formal and written details of the procedure for expressing work-related grievances and these should be provided as part of the conditions of service. In addition, employers are also legally required to name a person to whom grievances can be presented and the manner in which this must be done. The grievance procedure should also allow the staff member to appeal against any decision that results from them bringing a grievance to the attention of the organisation.

Discipline

It is important that the disciplinary process is not viewed purely as a punitive process. Although there will be some extreme cases where it is necessary to invoke disciplinary procedures in order to dismiss a member of staff, most activities carried out within the process should be aimed at changing behaviour so that the member of staff can make a greater contribution to the performance of the organisation. Thus, the main reason for disciplinary action is to encourage an employee whose standard of work or behaviour is unsatisfactory, to improve their performance (Rees and Porter, 2001).

Most organisations have accepted standards of behaviour, which are often outlined as the rules of the organisation. Although rules are not a legal obligation, it is important to ensure that all members of staff know what behaviour is acceptable or unacceptable to the organisation. They must be written down, non-discriminatory and agreed by staff representatives or unions.

The precise nature and content of the rules of the organisation will depend on three factors. First, the type of work done at the establishment will dictate what is important to the organisation and therefore what is considered to be acceptable behaviour. For example, physical or verbal abuse of a customer will be unacceptable in a public sport and leisure service, as the latter's purpose is to provide services to all members of the general public. In addition, racist or sexist jokes will also be unacceptable when providing equal opportunities for sport and leisure. The working conditions are also important and a hazardous occupation will be affected by more rules than a non-hazardous one; for example, there are likely to be more rules about health and safety affecting cafeteria staff than reception staff. Finally, the size of the organisation will make a difference in that the bigger the organisation, the more rules there will be, with more formal enforcement and with stricter penalties.

Although disciplinary rules are not statutory, a disciplinary procedure is. All organisations must provide staff with a written statement of the disciplinary rules that relate to an individual or outline where these rules can be seen. Organisations must also provide the name or description of a person to whom staff may apply if dissatisfied with any disciplinary decision, and the manner in which any such application should be made.

Disciplinary procedures usually include three stages. The first of these stages is the *verbal warning* stage when an individual is warned verbally about aspects of their behaviour that are considered to be unacceptable. This is followed by the *written warning* stage, which is invoked if behaviour does not change, or in cases of misconduct severe enough to omit the first stage. If the misconduct continues, a *final written warning* is issued where it is made clear that further misconduct will invoke severe penalties, such as dismissal or transfer.

Although the three stages differ in their severity and significance, the processes involved are similar. Individuals must be informed of the complaints against them and be given the opportunity to state their case before decisions are reached. The matter must be dealt with quickly and at each stage the consequence of not changing behaviour must be clearly outlined. Employees should be left in no doubt as to what action is being taken under the disciplinary procedure and what the consequences are. In addition, individuals should have the right to be accompanied at any interview by a friend or staff representative and they must also have the right to appeal against the decision.

Employees have the right to express genuine grievances and the law requires organisations to provide procedures in order for them to do this. In addition, the organisation has the right to ask its staff to behave in an acceptable manner, as long as the expectations of the organisation are reasonable. Although both grievance and discipline are often viewed as negative processes, both have much to offer public sport and leisure services and their staff. Genuine grievances will allow the organisation to improve its practices, making it a more equal organisation, while disciplinary procedures allow staff to improve their level of performance, which in turn benefits the organisation.

Managing outreach workers

One of the distinguishing features of the public sport and leisure industry is the relatively high proportion of employees that can be considered to be 'external workers'. Known as outreach workers or development staff, these employees work outside the main facilities of the local authority, either working directly with community groups or providing services from small community facilities, such as parish halls or schools. The type of services they offer are varied, but include sports coaching, providing activities for schoolchildren or activities for those who would rather not use the main facilities.

The employment of this type of staff makes public sport and leisure services much more flexible and appropriate to the needs of the community. Outreach workers should be employed, developed and disciplined in the same manner as staff employed to work in main facilities; however, there are a number of issues that need to be considered when managing such staff. These are:

- *Identity*: It is important that outreach workers are seen to be part of the local authority so that the general public are aware of the extent of the public sport and leisure service. In addition, association with the authority will give the employee status and authority in the eyes of the groups with which they work. Conversely, customers will also know that the service being provided has been planned, is funded and is safe.

The main way of building this identity is through the use of uniforms, name badges or cars with logos.

- *Communication*: Communication between managers and outreach workers can be somewhat complex, as managers are unlikely to see staff members on a daily basis to pass on information. In addition, staff will not see notice boards, will be delayed in receiving memos and will miss out on the general discussion or 'grapevine' that is associated with every workplace. As a result, managers have to make special efforts to ensure that outreach workers are as informed as quickly as staff who are employed in the main facilities. The use of mobile phones and e-mail has assisted greatly with the process of communication.

- *Control*: As outreach workers work predominantly on their own, away from day-to-day managerial guidance, it is important that mechanisms that control and guide the activities of the employee are in place. Although this sounds a little draconian, public sport and leisure managers must be confident that their staff are working in a manner that is appropriate for their job and that they are achieving targets. The main control mechanisms are work plans and monthly meetings where the manager and the staff member discuss the work that has been done and that they intend to do. These mechanisms also protect the outreach worker as they provide an opportunity to ask for assistance and feedback and for problems to be discussed.

- *Support*: More importantly, these meetings provide a means of support for people who are working in the field. This is important because outreach workers need to have the backing of their manager and the local authority in order to make decisions about programmed activities and resources. Support also assists with *motivation* and overcoming feelings of *isolation*.

- *Isolation*: Many outreach workers find that their job often leaves them feeling isolated from the main public sport and leisure service. As this will, in the long term, lead to a decrease in motivation, managers need to find ways of ensuring that their staff do not feel alienated. The regular meetings outlined above will assist with this, as will regular communication. Most importantly, however, it is important that outreach staff feel that they are part of the sport and leisure service and are part of a team. The main way of ensuring that this happens is to hold regular team meetings involving all outreach staff and their managers.

Summary and conclusions

This chapter has considered the role and practices of the function of human resource management, outlining the major issues that affect the management of people in public sport and leisure services. Primarily as a result of equal opportunities legislation and employment law, it is apparent that there is likely to be little difference between the HRM practices of the commercial and public sport and leisure sectors. Any differences in practice will be between organisations that value staff and those that do not, rather than sectoral differences. Having noted the role of legislation, it is, however, the responsibility of managers to take control of the selection, development and discipline of all staff that they manage. This chapter has outlined some of the techniques and processes that can assist with this vital function.

Suggested tasks for further study

- Identify a source of up-to-date information on employment law and equal opportunities.
- Evaluate a public sport and leisure services job advertisement against the criteria outlined in this chapter.
- Get a job description and use it to develop a person specification.
- Make a list of the items that should be included in the induction of a new pool lifeguard.

Further reading

Critten, P. (1994) *Human Resource Management in the Leisure Industry*, Harlow: Longman.

6 Financial management

This chapter was written by Simon Shibli of Sheffield Hallam University *

The introduction of Best Value has required managers to be able to demonstrate the efficiency and effectiveness of their services. The management techniques discussed in this section of the book help to deliver this efficiency and effectiveness, but arguably, the means of proving this lies in the financial arena. The purpose of this chapter is to illustrate how important techniques from the fields of financial accounting and management accounting can be usefully applied to the management of public services. After defining some of the key terms that are applicable to the field of financial management, the chapter will demonstrate the applicability of selected strategic, financial accounting and management accounting models and techniques to public sport and leisure management.

Terminology

There are no uniformly agreed definitions of key financial terms. In reality they vary according to the book they are taken from, or the context in which they are used. For the purposes of this chapter, easily understood and authoritative definitions are used. Where this is not possible, common definitions which convey the essentials of what is meant by a particular term in the context of public provision are used.

Strategic *financial management* is defined as 'the application of financial techniques to strategic decisions in order to help achieve the decision-maker's objectives' (www.axiom-e.co.uk/index, 2002). Strategic decisions are those which affect the whole organisation, take into account factors in the external environment and refer to the longer-term (five years or more) direction of an organisation. Strategic financial management requires the existence of objectives and acknowledges that financial techniques are an integral part of policy making and control.

* Except for Figure 6.1, all figures and tables in this chapter have been compiled by the contributing author, using his own data.

A second important definition is that of *financial accounting*, which is defined as:

> the classification and recording of monetary transactions of an entity in accordance with established concepts, principles, accounting standards and legal requirements, and their presentation, by means of profit and loss accounts, balance sheets and cash-flow statements, during and at the end of an accounting period.
>
> (Chartered Institute of Management Accountants (CIMA), 1996)

There are three points to note concerning this definition of financial accounting. First, financial accounting is concerned with the relatively passive activity of recording and classifying financial transactions. Second, financial accounting is governed by a series of prescribed procedures ranging from *established concepts* through to *legal requirements*. Third, the presentation of the results of financial accounting is in a specified form, such as the profit and loss account, balance sheet and cash-flow statement, which are known collectively as *financial statements*.

What the definition does not reveal is that it is a legal requirement for local authorities and limited companies to carry out financial accounting and in the case of limited companies the resulting financial statements must be filed with Companies House within a set period of an organisation's year end. Often the published accounts will be the only financial information available in the public domain about the entity.

A third key term is *management accounting*, which is defined by CIMA (1996) as:

> the process of identification, measurement, accumulation, analysis, preparation, interpretation and communication of information used by management to plan, evaluate and control within an entity and to assure appropriate use of and accountability for its resources.

There are also three points to note concerning the definition of management accounting. First, compared with financial accounting, management accounting involves being proactive. The information generated by management accounting is used for planning, decision making and control, whereas financial accounting data is used for reporting on an historical basis. Second, management accounting is compiled and reported in a way which best suits the needs of an organisation, rather than in the prescribed formats used in financial accounting. Third, management accounting is concerned with the efficient and effective use of resources, managed by the use of performance indicators which are discussed in the following chapter.

It therefore follows that meaningful assessments of whether a manager has been efficient and effective is most likely to be determined using management accounting techniques. However, unlike financial accounting data which is in the public domain, there are no legal requirements to give external users access to management accounting data. Arguably, the most useful information remains in-house.

In reality, financial accounting and management accounting are two sides of the same coin. Managers are required by law to record financial transactions according to the rules of financial accounting. However, no credible manager will plan to record financial transactions and wait to see what happens after a year. In practice, good managers plan their operations so as to achieve a desired outcome. The only way to achieve a desired outcome is to plan and control the service, using management accounting techniques.

Planning and control are achieved by techniques such as budgeting, variance analysis, breakeven analysis, and capital investment appraisal. These techniques are some, but not all, of the disciplines found within management accounting. Therefore there is a direct link between financial accounting and management accounting. The term *financial management* could quite legitimately be described as the application of financial accounting and management accounting techniques to the management of an organisation. It is in this sense that the term financial management is used in this chapter.

The role of strategic financial management in public sport and leisure provision

To test the applicability of strategic financial management to public sport and leisure services, it is worth examining the strategy model proposed by Sims and Smith (2000). A diagram of this simple model is shown in Figure 6.1.

Sims and Smith (2000) have proposed that the *competitive strategy* of a business concerns the services provided and the customers the organisation wishes to attract. Customers provide earnings (profits), which in turn gen-

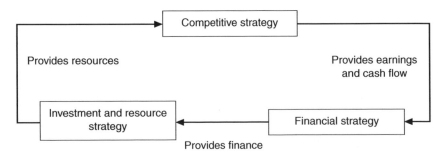

Figure 6.1 The three elements of strategy.
Source: Adapted from Sims and Smith, 2000.

crate cash. To prioritise the use of cash, a *financial strategy* exists which determines how much cash should be taken out of the business to reward key stakeholders and how much should be retained to help develop the future competitive strategy. The money which is retained within the business will have many competing uses, such as developing new services, buying new equipment, repairs and maintenance. Therefore an *investment and resource strategy* should exist to determine the best use of any cash generated for future use within the business.

It is important to consider the applicability of the model from a public sport and leisure perspective. The customers of these services are the fee-paying public and funding organisations who are prepared to buy into the policies pursued by a given provider. For example, rather than the National Health Service providing sports facilities, it might be more cost-effective to grant-aid public or indeed commercial sector organisations to provide this service on behalf of the NHS. This is a good example of how sport and leisure managers respond to developments in the external environment. Medical research suggests that in some instances cardiovascular exercise can be beneficial. Some doctors accept these findings and prescribe exercise rather than drugs. Public providers have identified this as a business opportunity and some take advantage of the referral to offer discounted use of facilities to those who are referred by their GP (doctor in general practice). As a result, despite the discount, there is an increase in the inward flow of cash.

In the public sector it is not the practice to distribute surplus funds externally, which might question the validity of having a financial strategy. However, it is possible for the surplus of one sport and leisure facility to be used to offset the overspend of another, or indeed for the overspend of one department in the authority to be offset by the surplus of another. Therefore it is prudent for services and departments to have a financial strategy. If managers are unable to demonstrate convincingly what they plan to do with their resources, they run the risk of having them diverted to people who can.

Assuming that some or all of any surpluses can be retained to help develop the competitive strategy, then a service needs to have an investment and resource strategy to determine the optimum use of surplus cash. This might be extra opening hours, taking on more staff, investing in information technology or other equipment or more outreach work. The important point is that for a given level of extra resource there needs to be a clear plan in place to obtain optimum benefit from it. Thus, although it might be in a slightly adapted format, the Sims and Smith (2000) model is applicable to public sport and leisure management and strategic financial management is confirmed as a requisite skill for those managing these services and those responsible for managing any external contractors.

The role of financial accounting in public sport and leisure provision

As explained in the terminology section above, financial accounting uses a combination of concepts and rules to produce financial statements in a standardised form. There are two common uses of financial accounting data that managers are likely to encounter. First, financial statements can be used to explain in-house financial performance. For example, the manager of a theatre could use its financial statements as evidence of the organisation's overall financial performance and health. Second, financial statements are often the only publicly available information from which to make a diagnosis of the financial health of other organisations. It is no coincidence that when vetting potential contractors bidding to manage public sport and leisure facilities, one of the tender submission requirements is usually three to five years' worth of financial statements. This is because it is considered possible to make a diagnosis about an organisation's financial health from its profit and loss account, balance sheet and cash-flow statement. Typical questions might include: *Can it afford to pay its bills? Does it have sufficient financial resources to be able to borrow funds to invest in new equipment?* Careful use of financial accounting data can be used to report internal performance and to make diagnoses of external organisations.

There are two fundamental questions that any analyst would like to answer when looking at a set of financial statements (Barker and Wilkinson-Riddle 1998). First, *Is the selling price higher than the cost?* For the public sector where the selling price is quite often lower than the cost, because of local authority subsidy, the first question can be modified to *Is the organisation operating within the resources allocated to it?* The answer to the first question can be found on the profit and loss account. Second, *Is the organisation well set to carry on trading?* The second question aims to establish if the organisation can pay its bills and if it is in control of its assets. The answer to the second question can be found on the balance sheet.

Information from the profit and loss account

The profit and loss account is an analysis of how the capital or net worth of an organisation has changed over a given period. This point can be illustrated by a quick overview of the data set out in Table 6.1. In Year 2003, a sports centre generated £900,000 worth of income (turnover) of which £650,000 was used on the direct costs of providing the service (cost of sales) leaving a gross profit of £250,000. A further £190,000 worth of administrative expenses (indirect expenditure) was offset against the gross profit, leaving a pre-tax profit of £60,000.

As it is part of the public sector, the organisation is exempt from paying tax and therefore the retained profit for the year was £60,000. To illustrate how the profit and loss account is an analysis of how the organisation's capital has changed, the bottom line of the profit and loss account in Table 6.1 can be summarised as meaning *At the end of 2003 the organisation had £60,000 of extra resources* [not necessarily cash] *available to it compared with the same time last year.*

The first question has been answered, that is, the selling price was higher than the cost, or alternatively the organisation operated within the resources allocated to it. It is customary for financial statements to contain the data for two years' worth of trading activity – the year in question and the comparative figures for the previous year. Therefore a follow-up question might be *How does this year's performance compare with last year?* In this case, in Year 2003 a £60,000 profit was made, whereas in Year 2002 the profit was £27,000. In simple terms it can be concluded that this year's performance has been an improvement on last year.

Having assessed the basic indicators, the next important question is *How does this year's actual performance compare with planned performance?* If the organisation concerned had planned to make a profit of £45,000, then clearly a surplus of £60,000 demonstrates that not only has the organisation operated within its resources, but in financial terms it has also been more effective than expected. Equally, had the profit target been £100,000 then, despite operating within its resources, the organisation would have been relatively ineffective because actual performance was £40,000 less than planned performance. Unfortunately, financial statements tend not to reveal planned performance and therefore in the absence of internal management accounting data, financial statements tend to be limited to making broad-brush common sense analyses.

All organisations, including public organisations, need to grow. This may seem to be a sweeping generalisation; however, the reality is that with the effects of inflation it is necessary for organisations to grow simply to maintain their position. For example, staff are the largest single expense in public provision and most staff will be on local government pay scales which can lead to two pay rises per year; an incremental rise and a cost of living (inflation) rise. It is also rare for other expenditure (for example, on premises, utilities or marketing) to remain static over time and these too

Table 6.1 Sports centre profit and loss account

	2003 £	2002 £
Turnover	900,000	850,000
Cost of sales	650,000	638,000
Gross profit	250,000	212,000
Administrative expenses	190,000	185,000
Pre-tax profit for year	60,000	27,000
Taxation	0	0
Retained profit for year	60,000	27,000

tend to increase. Thus, if an organisation wishes to maintain the desirable equilibrium of operating within its resources, it has to grow to keep pace with its increased costs.

Measuring growth

Measuring growth can be achieved by using what is known as horizontal or year-on-year analysis. Table 6.2 shows the data from Table 6.1, subjected to horizontal (year-on-year) analysis.

The growth calculation involves two parts. First, it is necessary to calculate the change in each component of the profit and loss account (this year minus last year) and second, to express the change as a percentage of last year. Thus, in Table 6.2, the absolute increase in turnover is £50,000, which is a 6 per cent increase on the previous year. Signs of successful growth are an increase in turnover and an increase in profit. In the case of Table 6.2, turnover increased by 6 per cent and profits increased by 122 per cent, which is clearly a sign of successful growth.

A second way of analysing financial statements is using common size or vertical analysis, where a key variable – usually turnover – is given a value of 100 per cent and all other lines on the profit and loss account are expressed as a percentage of this key variable. It is less complicated than it sounds and an example can be seen in Table 6.3.

Looking at Table 6.3, in 2003 for every £1 of turnover, 28p was left over as gross profit (common size of gross profit is 28 per cent), whereas in 2002 for every £1 of turnover only 25p was left over as gross profit (common size of gross profit is 25 per cent). This is a good example of how efficiency has improved at the gross profit level. That is, for each £1 of input (turnover), there is a higher level of output (gross profit) than there was in 2002. Therefore the organisation can be said to have become more efficient. The same logic holds true for the bottom line, *retained profit for the year*. For every £1 of turnover, 7p is left over as retained profit, whereas in the previous year retained profit was only 3p per £1 of turnover. Thus, at the retained profit level the organisation has also become more efficient.

Table 6.2 Profit and loss account horizontal analysis

	2003	2002	Change	% Change
Turnover	900,000	850,000	50,000	6
Cost of sales	650,000	638,000	12,000	2
Gross profit	250,000	212,000	38,000	18
Administrative expenses	190,000	185,000	5,000	3
Pre-tax profit for year	60,000	27,000	33,000	122
Taxation	0	0	0	0
Retained profit for year	60,000	27,000	33,000	122

Table 6.3 Profit and loss account vertical analysis

	2003	Common size (%)	2002	Common size (%)
Turnover	900,000	100	850,000	100
Cost of sales	650,000	72	638,000	75
Gross profit	250,000	28	212,000	25
Administrative expenses	190,000	21	185,000	22
Pre-tax profit for year	60,000	7	27,000	3
Taxation	0	0	0	0
Retained profit for year	60,000	7	27,000	3

After considering Tables 6.2 and 6.3 together, it can be concluded that the organisation has become more efficient because as turnover has increased (6 per cent), costs (cost of sales and administrative expenses) have increased at a lower rate (2 per cent and 3 per cent respectively). Thus, in simple terms, and in the absence of any other data such as an organisation's business plan, it is possible to obtain useful findings about an organisation's financial performance from its published profit and loss account.

Many public sport and leisure organisations do not exist to make a profit and managers might legitimately query the relevance of Table 6.3. However, many of the mainstream analysis models which exist can be adapted to suit the needs of a particular context. Table 6.4 outlines a tool that is particularly useful for public managers, that of recovery rate analysis. Recovery rate analysis indicates how much of the costs of running the service is recovered by the income it generates and is a key indicator of efficiency as it demonstrates how successful a manager has been at controlling organisational costs in proportion to the revenue earned. Recovery rate is defined as the percentage of total expenditure 'recovered' by earned income. For example, if a swimming pool's earned income was £350,000 and the total cost of providing the facility was £500,000, then the recovery rate would be $((350,000 \div 500,000) \times 100) = 70$ per cent.

Table 6.4 Recovery rate analysis

	2003	Common size (%)	2002	Common size (%)
Admission revenue	125,000	63	100,000	52
Catering/vending	11,000	6	7,000	4
Earned income	136,000	68	107,000	56
Total expenditure	200,000	100	192,000	100
Deficit	−64,000	−32	−85,000	−44
Council grant	64,000	32	85,000	44
Net financial performance	0	0	0	0

Unlike Tables 6.2 and 6.3, Table 6.4 takes total expenditure as its base figure (100 per cent) and expresses all other variables as a proportion of this key variable. The key point is that earned income as a percentage of total expenditure has increased from 56 per cent in 2002 to 68 per cent in 2003. In other words the centre has become more efficient as it requires less input (council subsidy) to achieve its output.

Information available from the balance sheet

The second question, *Is the business well set to continue trading?*, can in part be obtained from analysis of the balance sheet. Reading, interpreting and explaining a balance sheet is not solely the domain of trained accountants and managers should be able to identify and articulate the meaning of a balance sheet. The purpose of a balance sheet is to put a value on the net worth of an organisation. To do this requires a list of those things of value (assets) which the organisation owns, such as buildings and cash; and a list of those things the organisation owes to others (liabilities), such as loans or creditors. The difference between these two figures is the *capital*, *net worth*, or *equity* of the business.

For example, if a house is worth £250,000 and the mortgage is £60,000, then the owner's capital (net worth) is £190,000 (£250,000 minus £60,000). A balance sheet is a slightly more complicated way of applying the same logic to an organisation. To illustrate the point, Table 6.5 shows the balance sheet for the same organisation whose profit and loss account was featured in the tables above.

The main difference between Table 6.5 and the house/mortgage example given above is that balance sheets make a distinction between fixed assets, current assets and current creditors. In simple terms, on a balance sheet the *fixed* means of long-term value to an organisation (i.e. two years or more) is part of the organisation's infrastructure and not regularly traded on a day-to-day basis. Sports centres hope to use gym equipment for more than two years and the purchase and sale of gym equipment is not a regular part of their activities. Therefore gym equipment is a fixed asset. By contrast, organisations hope to convert stock and debtors into cash within a year and certain creditors need to be paid within a year. Anything which is planned to be converted into cash or paid within one year is said to be *current*. Thus, in Table 6.5, assets minus creditors equals £452,000 which in turn is the net worth of the organisation.

In the above table, the opening capital for 2003 was £392,000, that is, the value of the capital at the end of 2002. The difference in capital between 2003 and 2002 is £452,000 minus £392,000, which equals £60,000. This figure is not a coincidence. The organisation's profit and loss account, in Tables 6.1, 6.2 and 6.3, details a profit of £60,000 and the definition of the profit and loss account is an analysis of how capital has

Table 6.5 Sports centre balance sheet

	2003	2002
Fixed assets		
Buildings	350,000	330,000
Equipment	95,000	60,000
Total fixed assets	445,000	390,000
Current assets		
Stock	5,000	4,000
Debtors	2,500	1,500
Cash	37,500	20,500
Total current assets	45,000	26,000
Current creditors		
Creditors payable within 1 year	38,000	24,000
Net current assets	7,000	2,000
Net assets	452,000	392,000
Capital		
Ordinary Shares	100,000	100,000
Profit and loss account	352,000	292,000
TOTAL CAPITAL	452,000	392,000

changed. Therefore there is a direct link between the balance sheet and the profit and loss account in that the profit and loss account 'explains' how the balance sheet has changed.

Ratio analysis

Two of the determinants of whether a business is well set to continue trading are the ability to pay its bills and the degree of control it has over its assets. The ability to pay debts as they fall due is called *liquidity* and is measured by liquidity ratios. Liquidity ratios compare the amount of current assets available to pay current creditors. The first of these is called the current ratio and simply compares total current assets with total current creditors.

Current ratio calculation

	2003	2002
Current assets	45,000	26,000
Current creditors	38,000	24,000
Current ratio	1.18:1[1]	1.08:1

1 (45,000 / 38,000):1

The current ratio calculation shows that in 2003, for every £1 of current creditors, the organisation had £1.18 in current assets. This finding suggests that the organisation can meet its bills. Furthermore, comparison with 2002 indicates that there has been a marginal improvement in liquidity from 1.08:1 to 1.18:1.

It is sometimes the case that organisations are unable to sell their stock as quickly as they would like, which in turn questions the validity of including stock as part of current assets for the purposes of testing liquidity. To compensate for this, a second ratio called the *acid test* or *quick ratio* can be calculated to see the extent to which an organisation is dependent on selling stock for its liquidity.

Acid test ratio calculation

	2003	2002
Current assets	45,000	26,000
minus stock	(5,000)	(4,000)
Equals	40,000	22,000
Current creditors	38,000	24,000
Acid test ratio[1]	1.05:1	0.92:1

1 (40,000 / 38,000):1

The acid test ratio reveals that in 2003 the organisation still had sufficient resources to meet current creditors, whereas in 2002, once stock is taken out of the equation there was only 92p available to meet every £1 of current creditors. Liquidity ratios of at least 1:1 would be regarded as being a prudent level of liquidity. Once a liquidity ratio falls below 1:1, further clarification might be necessary from an organisation's management concerning their strategy for being able to settle debts as they fall due.

Liquidity tests are one of the ways in which managers can assess the creditworthiness of potential business contacts. If a local authority contracts a commercial organisation to manage sports centres on its behalf, the contractor acts as the agent of the local authority. The local authority does not want its reputation to be damaged by the actions of its agents and would therefore be well advised to check the organisation's financial statements to ensure that they are capable of paying their bills. Similarly, at unit level a sports centre manager or theatre manager might consider hiring out their venue for an exhibition or conference. Whether agreeing to hire out a venue proves to be a good or bad decision depends in part on whether or not full payment is received for the services offered. Credit terms might be offered to an organisation with a strong balance sheet and prudent liquidity levels, whereas a hirer without such credentials might be required to pay in advance.

The extent to which an organisation is in control of its assets can be measured by the 'debt ratio', which is a measure of the extent to which an organisation's assets are funded by creditors. To illustrate the point, consider the case of two house owners who both have houses worth £250,000. Owner A has a mortgage for £60,000 and Owner B has a mortgage for £225,000. Common sense suggests that Owner A is in a better position than Owner B, but how can the relationship be quantified to prove the point?

	Owner A	*Owner B*
House (asset)	250,000	250,000
Mortgage (creditor)	60,000	225,000
Net worth (equity)	190,000	25,000

The debt ratio measures the extent to which assets are funded by debts, so the debt ratio for each owner would be:

	Owner A	*Owner B*
House (asset)	250,000	250,000
Mortgage	60,000	225,000
Debt ratio[1]	24%	90%

1 Debt ratio = (Creditors / Assets) $\times$ 100

Applying the same logic to Table 6.5, the debt ratio for each year would be:

	2003	*2002*
Fixed assets	445,000	390,000
Current assets	45,000	416,000
Total assets	490,000	416,000
Total creditors	38,000	24,000
Debt ratio	8%	6%

A debt ratio of 8 per cent for 2003 and 6 per cent for 2002 reveals that the organisation has very low levels of debt and therefore controls the vast majority of its assets. Organisations with high debt ratios can, in effect, be controlled by their creditors. For example, if a balance sheet reveals very high levels of borrowing, it may well be that the banks and other providers of funds are the real controllers of the organisation, rather than the owners. It could be a mistake to appoint commercial contractors to manage a sports centre only to discover that the contractor was at the mercy of banks who were exercising a controlling influence.

There are many more ratios and analysis techniques that can be used to assess the financial statements of organisations. However, this section of the chapter has focused on the basic areas that public sport and leisure managers should investigate. Calculating ratios and interpreting them should not be viewed as an end point, but rather as the basis for subsequent investigation and clarification.

Benchmarking

A topical application of financial accounting that is specific to public provision is benchmarking, which will be discussed in the following chapter. In terms of demonstrating efficiency, innovation and customer orientation in the Best Value climate of greater transparency, local authorities are required to 'benchmark' their performance against other authorities and providers from the voluntary and commercial sectors. There are numerous variables from financial data that could be benchmarked and Figure 6.2 considers turnover. If sports centres of comparable type, size, opening hours and programmes benchmarked their turnover data, the result might look like that shown in Figure 6.2.

The median score for turnover is approximately £750,000 and centres achieving less than this might wish to investigate why they are performing below the median. Equally, 34 of the 40 centres might like to know how the top six centres achieved a turnover in excess of £1m. It is only by identifying performance and making it public that managers and authorities can learn from each other. Benchmarking can be applied to a vast array of financial accounting data and other priorities might be profitability, recov-

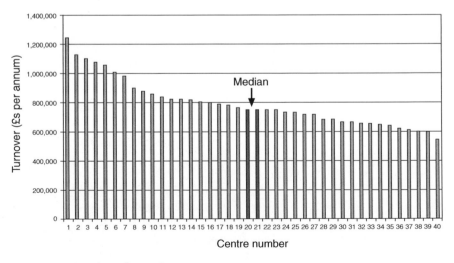

Figure 6.2 Benchmarking of turnover.

ery rate, total expenditure, liquidity, debt ratio and total capital. To be able to make sense of the data that benchmarking provides, managers must have a basic grasp of financial accounting data and what such data means.

The core skills needed in financial accounting are the ability to understand what financial statements mean and to be conversant in what is regarded as the language of business. It can be argued that although managers are unlikely to have day-to-day responsibility for recording financial transactions, the skill that they do need is the ability to analyse, interpret and explain financial accounting data. There are two key reasons for this. First, they need to be able to communicate internal performance to external stakeholders and, second, managers need to be able to make common-sense diagnoses of other organisations from their financial statements. Benchmarking, the discipline of comparing an organisation's performance against other organisations, integrates these two uses of financial accounting data, which in turn can be used as the building blocks for continuous improvement.

The role of management accounting in public sport and leisure provision

The role of management accounting is to provide managers with financial data for planning, decision making and control purposes. In public sport and leisure provision the most fundamental use of management accounting is budgeting; that is, expressing the organisation's business objectives in financial terms. Without such planning, what is intended to occur (effectiveness) and what actually happens is left to chance.

As discussed in Chapter 4, good practice suggests that managers should have a clear statement of what they wish to achieve and should put in place a plan that will enable them to deliver it. In addition, actual performance should be regularly monitored against the plan so that, if necessary, corrective action can be taken to ensure consistency between actual performance and planned performance. To illustrate the point, Table 6.6 develops the data used in Tables 6.1, 6.2 and 6.3 to demonstrate how simple management accounting techniques, such as budgeting, can be used to convert relatively passive financial data into genuinely useful information.

In Table 6.6, the data in the 'Actual' column is financial accounting data, whereas the figures in *italics* are management accounting data. Unlike in Tables 6.1, 6.2 and 6.3, it is now possible to diagnose how effective the organisation has been in financial terms. Although the organisation made a profit of £60,000, a profit of £90,000 was planned to be made and therefore in financial terms the organisation has been ineffective. The reason why the budgeted target was not met was that, despite turnover being £25,000 more than expected, costs were £55,000 more

Table 6.6 Actual versus budget comparison

	Actual	Budget	Variance[1]	Direction[2]	Percentage[3]
Turnover	900,000	875,000	25,000	F	103
Cost of sales	650,000	600,000	50,000	U	108
Gross profit	250,000	275,000	25,000	U	91
Administrative expenses	190,000	185,000	5,000	U	103
Pre-tax profit for year	60,000	90,000	−30,000	U	67

Notes
1 Variance = Actual minus Budget
2 Direction F = Favourable, U = Unfavourable
3 Percentage = (Actual /Budget) × 100

than expected, leading to an unfavourable net profit variance of £30,000. The added value of management accounting in this instance is that not only does it quantify how much actual performance has deviated from the plan, but it also gives an insight into why.

Assuming that the data in Table 6.6 was available on a regular basis, such as monthly, then it becomes possible to take corrective action once deviations between planned performance and actual performance have been noted. The longer the lead time managers have between identifying problems and doing something about them, the greater the probability of taking effective corrective action. One of the problems facing public sport and leisure managers is that often the information they require is received so much in arrears of actual events that it is not possible to take corrective action.

A further feature of management accounting data is that its use is not solely confined to purely financial data; it can be used on other quantitative data, such as admissions data. Table 6.7 expands the data in Table 6.6 by including the actual and budgeted number of admissions.

Analysis of the admissions data reveals further evidence of why the organisation failed to achieve its financial targets. It was planned to

Table 6.7 Analysis of admissions data

	Actual	Budget	Variance	Direction	Percentage
Turnover	900,000	875,000	25,000	F	103
Cost of sales	650,000	600,000	50,000	U	108
Gross profit	250,000	275,000	25,000	U	91
Administrative expenses	190,000	185,000	5,000	U	103
Pre-tax profit for year	60,000	90,000	30,000	U	67
Admissions	*375,000*	*350,000*	*25,000*	*F*	*107*
Average spend per head	*£2.40*	*£2.50*	*−£0.10*	*U*	*96*

'extract' £2.50 per admission, whereas in practice, the actual extraction rate was £2.40. Spread over 375,000 admissions, a shortfall of 10p per admission equals £37,500 – more than enough to make up the difference between actual and planned performance. By making use of this type of analysis the focus of enquiry can be made even more specific, that is, *Why was average spend per head 10p less than expected?* Possible reasons might include running out of stock, having insufficient staff to service the extra admissions or having insufficient change for vending machines. Each line of enquiry enables a clearer diagnosis of the problem to be made, so that eventually the cause or causes of under-performance can be identified and rectified.

Costs

At a more strategic level than budgeting, management accounting techniques can be used to inform the overall direction of an organisation through an understanding of the nature and behaviour of costs. Costs can be classified into fixed, variable and semi-variable costs. Fixed costs do not vary in the short term relative to the number of admissions achieved in a facility or in relation to opening hours. For example, salaries, rent, rates and insurance will not alter in response to changes in customer throughput or variations in opening hours.

By contrast, variable costs do alter in relation to admissions and opening hours. In the case of a swimming pool, the cost of issuing customers with a wristband varies in direct proportion to the number of customers. Semi-variable costs contain an element of fixed cost and an element of variable cost. A telephone line costs around £30 per quarter to rent regardless of how often the telephone is used. The more it is used, the more expense is incurred in terms of telephone units; that is, the variable element of the cost changes in proportion to how many calls are made. The crucial point, however, is that for a given level of opening hours in a facility, costs will be either fixed or variable.

The example of a 25-metre swimming pool will be used to illustrate cost behaviour in practice and more importantly to demonstrate how an understanding of cost behaviour can be used to inform management decision making. On average the pool achieves 2,000 admissions per week at a price of £3.50 per admission. The variable costs per swim such as wristbands and ticketing cost 6p per admission and the fixed costs per week are £6,500. Using these pieces of information that managers should know, it is possible to derive information that can assist decision making. A systematic way of using this is by a marginal costing matrix, such as that shown in Figure 6.3. It is worth noting, however, that the marginal costing matrix cannot make decisions for managers, but it can help to inform decision making by modelling the likely effects of management decisions.

Quantity 2,000	Selling price £3.50	Revenue £7,000		
	Variable cost £0.06	Total variable cost £120		
	Contribution £3.44	Total contribution £6,880	Contribution/sales ratio 98%	
		Fixed cost £6,500	Breakeven units 1,890	Breakeven sales £6,613
		Net profit £380	Margin of safety (units) 110	Margin of safety (sales) £387

Figure 6.3 Marginal costing matrix.

Using the data given in Figure 6.3, the marginal costing matrix is built up as follows:

1 Admissions (2,000) × Price (£3.50) = Total Revenue (£7,000)
2 Admissions (2,000) × Variable Cost per Swim (£0.06) = Total Variable Cost (£120)
3 Total Revenue (£7,000) − Total Variable Cost (£120) = Total Contribution[1] (£6,880)
4 (Total Contribution (£6,880) ÷ Total Revenue (7,000)) × 100 = Contribution to Sales Ratio 98 per cent, i.e. 98 per cent of the admission price is contributed towards fixed costs
5 Total Contribution (£6,880) − Fixed Costs (£6,500) = Net Profit (£380)

If each admission contributed £3.44 towards fixed costs and fixed costs are £6,500 then the number of admissions required to cover fixed costs, or *breakeven*, is 6,500/3.44 which equals 1,890. Furthermore, if the pool is currently achieving 2,000 admissions per week and the breakeven position is 1,890, then the pool can afford to lose 110 admissions per week before it starts to make a loss. The number of admissions that can afford to be lost before the breakeven point is reached is known as the *margin of safety*. It can be expressed as a number of admissions (110), a level of sales (£387) or indeed as a percentage, in that the pool could afford to lose 5.5 per cent (110/2000) of its admissions before it starts to make a loss. This is a rather thin margin to be working with and should focus a manager's attention on the fact that the critical success factor in meeting budget is to

[1] Contribution = the amount of total revenue that 'contributed' towards fixed costs after subtracting variable costs.

make sure that the requisite number of admissions are achieved. Furthermore, managers should note that as virtually all of the costs are fixed (£6,880, as opposed to £120), the only way to grow the business is to achieve higher throughput, not to cut costs.

The basic marginal costing matrix outlined in Figure 6.3 can be developed to model the effects of management decisions so that the optimum decisions are made and poor decisions are avoided. For example, if a manager thought that demand for swimming could be stimulated by cutting the price and had suggested that a 50p cut in price would lead to an extra 200 admissions per week, would this be a good decision? One method of evaluating the recommendation would be to subject it to analysis using the marginal costing matrix.

Figure 6.4 shows a comparison of the base case data used in Figure 6.3 and, immediately underneath it, the effects of the *what if* scenario, that is reducing the price by 50p to increase admissions by 200 per week.

The effect of implementing the suggestion would be to convert the pool from profit making (£380 per week) to loss making (−£32 per week). The number of admissions required to break even would be 2,211 and therefore to prevent the recommendation from causing the pool to make a loss, the minimum increase in admissions would need to be 211. Even achieving an increase of 211 admissions would eliminate the pool's previous weekly profit of £380. Therefore in purely financial terms, the use of price cuts in this instance to stimulate demand would be a poor decision. However, if the aim was to pursue equity objectives and the extra admissions would be drawn from disadvantaged groups and the authority was prepared to accept elimination of profits in return for meeting social objectives; then the decision to cut prices as modelled in Figure 6.4 would be a good decision.

Following on from the marginal costing matrix, cost structures and their impact on strategy is the final topic considered in this chapter.

Quantity		Selling price	Revenue			
Base case	2,000	£3.50	£7,000			
'What if'	2,200	£3.00	£6,600			
		Variable cost	**Total variable cost**			
		£0.06	£120			
		£0.06	£132			
		Contribution	**Total contribution**	**Contribution/sales ratio**		
		£3.44	£6,880	98%		
		£2.94	£6,468	98%		
			Fixed cost	**Breakeven units**		**Breakeven sales**
			£6,500	1,890		£6,613
			£6,500	2,211		£6,633
			Net profit	**Margin of safety (units)**		**Margin of safety (sales)**
			£380	110		£387
			−£32	−11		−£33

Figure 6.4 Comparing base case with 'what if' scenario.

Traditionally, public sector managers have tried to deal with the imbalance between income and expenditure by trying to cut costs. There are, however, three ways in which imbalances can be rectified:

- reduce expenditure and maintain income at current levels;
- increase income and maintain expenditure at current levels;
- reduce expenditure and increase income as they are not mutually exclusive.

Whether or not any one of these strategies is better than the others depends upon the context in which a decision is being made and the cost structure of the organisation concerned.

Cost structure in this context means the balance between an organisation's fixed and variable costs and their behaviour in response to changes in levels of activity. In public services, for any given level of activity such as opening hours, the vast majority of costs are fixed. Salary costs are fixed and the cost of staff who are not salaried will be in effect fixed by the level of activity. For example, if a theatre box office is open for 60 hours of the week and requires 3 staff to be on duty at all times, then the cost of running the box office is $3 \times 60 = 180$ hours, at the hourly rate of box office staff. The only way in which this figure could change would be if opening hours were changed, for example to 50 hours per week, in which case the cost would be fixed at 150 hours of box office staff time per week.

In other businesses, such as restaurants, variable costs (the price of food, drink and to a certain extent staff) are a relatively high proportion of total costs. By serving more meals than planned, a restaurant's costs will increase significantly, as will its income. By the same logic, serving fewer meals than planned will cause costs to decrease significantly. As a result of different cost structures applying to different types of operation, the concept of *operational gearing* is a useful way of identifying logically correct strategies to employ in given circumstances. The term operational gearing is a measure of risk derived from the marginal costing matrix (Figures 6.3 and 6.4), which quantifies the ratio of contribution to profit.

Using the data in Figure 6.3, the operational gearing for the swimming pool would be $(6,880 / 380) = 18.1$. An operational gearing of 18.1 means that for every £18.10 of contribution, once fixed costs are subtracted, only £1 is left over as net profit. This implies that the organisation has very high fixed costs as a percentage of total costs and this should focus a manager's attention on the fact that ensuring admission figures are met is vitally important. It also suggests that the only logical way to grow the business is by increasing revenue and not by trying to cut costs.

Knowledge of the operational gearing ratio and the nature of cost behaviour in sport and leisure services suggests that the pursuit of a strategy of increased throughput and increased revenue per customer is a much more logical approach than trying to cut costs that do not vary in relation to the level of activity. This is the approach taken by Sheffield International Venues, as described in Figure 6.5.

Summary and conclusions

The purpose of this chapter was to demonstrate how techniques drawn from strategic financial management, financial accounting and management accounting have a role to play in the management of public sport and leisure services. Underpinning the rationale for why techniques from these disciplines are important are the twin factors of the increasing complexity of a manager's job and the convergence of the public sector and commercial sector management approaches. There are two main points to emerge from the chapter.

First, financial accounting is the language of business as it uses standardised approaches for reporting financial performance (profit and loss account) and financial position (balance sheet). As all limited companies and public organisations are required to report a summary of their financial transactions using financial accounting techniques, it follows that it is an essential skill to understand what these techniques are. As the public and commercial sectors now interact more than they have done previously, public managers need to be able to make assessments about potential partners as well as analysing and reporting on a partner's financial performance.

Second, the public sector operates in a climate of increased accountability caused by an emphasis on effectiveness, rather than economy. Managers need the skills to plan, make decisions and control their spheres of responsibility. The nature of cost and its behaviour in relation to activity levels determines that the most logical strategies are those which focus on increased customer throughput and customer expenditure, rather than cost cutting. Use of management accounting techniques will not replace decision making by humans, but when used properly they can provide the

---

Driven in part by the nature and behaviour of costs, Sheffield International Venues Limited (SIV), which manages most of the public sport and leisure facilities in Sheffield, offers unlimited access to a host of sports facilities such as gyms, swimming pools and running tracks for a direct debit subscription of around £20 per month to the 'Fitness Unlimited' scheme. Currently SIV collect approximately 8,000 direct debits per month and by some margin have the largest market share in Sheffield for health and fitness type activities. There has been such an increase in customer throughput at SIV venues that capacity has had to be increased to cope with the new levels of demand. The success of SIV's 'Fitness Unlimited' is an excellent example of a public sector provider focusing on revenue generation as its key strategy rather than cost cutting, having realised that for a given level of activity (opening hours) there is very little that can be done about the majority of costs.

Figure 6.5 Sheffield City Council.

basis from which the most effective decisions can be made. Although many decisions in public sport and leisure services will have a political dimension, management accounting techniques can be used to inform the political process by modelling the effects of decisions to ensure that these can be made using the best information available and with full awareness of their likely financial effects.

Public sport and leisure managers are required to have a much greater input into the performance of their service than previously. The role of management accounting techniques in assisting with this confirms that these techniques are an integral part of the public sector manager's portfolio of skills.

Suggested tasks for further study

- Obtain the published annual report and accounts of a public sector sport or leisure organisation in which you are interested. Imagine that you are the treasurer of the organisation and are required to present the accounts to the organisation's Annual General Meeting (AGM). What are the key points you would make and how would you substantiate these points with evidence?
- To what extent do you consider that the accounts of your chosen organisation (from the task above) enable you to make meaningful comments about the organisation's efficiency and effectiveness? Where do you identify information deficiencies and how would you obtain the information required?
- Using a local sports or leisure service as a case study and your knowledge of cost structures, explain how you would set about improving the organisation's bottom line (net profit). Justify your answer with reference to the logic underpinning your knowledge of cost structures and cost behaviour.

Further reading

Naylor, D.J. (2001) *Managing Your Leisure Service Budget*, London: Ravenswood Publications Limited.

7   Performance management

Since the introduction of Best Value, performance management has been at the top of the management agenda for those delivering public sport and leisure services. This is primarily because the Best Value and CPA frameworks are intended to be performance management frameworks and, as outlined in Chapter 4, it is important to note that performance management is intrinsically linked with strategy and planning. Strategy and planning activities set the objectives and establish the plans that the performance management process must deliver. Within the current public sector context, fundamental performance reviews generate the information that is integrated into the service performance management framework.

The performance management framework that public services are required to follow has previously been presented in Figure 2.2. This chapter focuses on the service level and discusses the need for performance management and its role in the delivery of public sport and leisure services. It considers issues relating to performance management and focuses, in detail, on performance measurement by discussing performance indicators and performance comparison.

Definitions and structures

Performance management can be defined as:

> a means of getting better results by understanding and managing performance within an agreed framework of planned goals, standards and competence requirements. It is also a process to establish a shared understanding about what is to be achieved.
>
> (Armstrong, 1999)

It is a series of processes and techniques and from this it is apparent that performance management is an integral part of the organisational strategy and planning process and as such, the performance management of public services fits into the framework promoted by Best Value.

Having defined performance management it is useful to identify two other commonly used terms of performance management. The first of these is *performance indicators* (PIs), which can be defined as 'a piece of empirical data representing performance that can be compared over time or with similar organisations' (Taylor *et al.*, 2000: p. 4). Examples might include the number of complaints, the number of users of a playground or the percentage of cost recovery. The second other key term is *target* and this can be considered to be a standard or level associated with the performance indicator. For example, increased access by ethnic minority groups might be the performance indicator and a 10 per cent increase is the target that managers should achieve.

A simplistic explanation of performance management can be provided by considering the control loop, outlined in Figure 7.1. Many management tasks involve managers putting an input, such as money or staff into a process – the service being delivered. These inputs might be adjusted if information regarding the outputs of the process indicates a need for change. This feedback is given by sensors that measure the output. Performance indicators perform this role in the management of services. This allows comparison of what should have been achieved, with what has been achieved (the target) and the manager then makes adjustments to the input or the process based on this. This, in simple terms, is performance management.

There are several reasons why performance must be managed and these reasons are particularly pertinent to public sport and leisure services. First, organisations need to demonstrate that public money has been spent as agreed and that resources have been used efficiently to achieve the

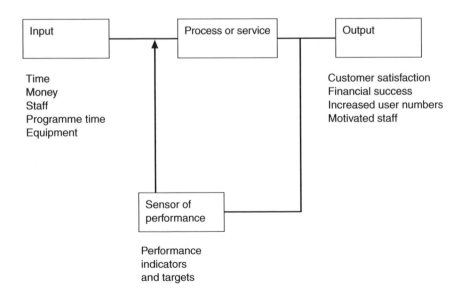

Figure 7.1 A control loop.

intended result. In addition, politicians are accountable for the policy decisions they make. Both sets of accountabilities require performance to be managed and measured. Second, performance management assists with meeting stakeholder expectations. Although complicated by the number of stakeholder groups that public services have, if managers set performance targets that are agreed by each group, they can then manage the service to meet these targets. Third, performance management requires managers to set intended results and then manage their services to meet these results. The concept of managing for results has become increasingly important in the public sector over the past two decades, primarily for the reasons outlined in Chapter 2. Finally, a performance management framework should incorporate the management of staff. This is necessary to ensure that results are achieved, as it is staff members who will make the difference as to whether targets are met. Thus, the management of individual performance in order to integrate organisational and individual performance is essential.

Performance management frameworks

In order to deliver services of best value, the Government has adopted five dimensions of performance (Audit Commission, 2000). These are:

- strategic objectives: why the service exists and what it seeks to achieve;
- cost/efficiency: the resources committed to a service and the efficiency with which they are turned into outputs;
- service delivery outcomes: how well the service is being operated in order to achieve the strategic objectives;
- quality: the quality of service delivered, explicitly reflecting users' experiences of services;
- fair access: ease and equality of access to services.

There are a number of performance management frameworks that are available to managers in order to focus on the above areas. Two of these, the EFQM Excellence Model and Quest are presented in Chapter 8, as their main focus is the quality of services. A third performance management framework is the Balanced Scorecard approach developed by Kaplan and Norton (1996), which focuses on four key aspects of the organisation and requires the measurement of these aspects. This approach emphasises the need to provide management with information that covers all relevant areas of performance, in an objective and unbiased fashion (ACCA, 2001).

The four key aspects of the Balanced Scorecard are:

- the customer: managers need to ask what existing and new customers value from the service. In addition, they need to identify potential customers and find out why they are not using the service. This allows targets that matter to customers to be developed and incorporated into the performance management system;

- internal: this considers the operations of the organisation in order to identify what has to be achieved to meet objectives. The purpose of this is to improve internal processes and decision making;
- innovation and learning: this requires managers to identify areas of improvement and to learn from past performance. This enables the organisation to identify its competitive position and to identify strengths and weaknesses that need incorporating into the planning process;
- financial: managers are required to consider the financing of the organisation in the context of creating value for stakeholders. Although finance has traditionally had a set of well-established performance measures and targets, the choice of which to use needs to be determined in consultation with key stakeholders.

The scorecard is balanced as managers are required to think in terms of all four areas of performance and to measure their performance in these areas. A key feature of this approach is that it considers both the internal and external aspects of the organisation, in particular customers. In addition, it should be related to the organisation's strategy as it considers operations in the light of organisational objectives. Finally, it focuses on both operational and social objectives of the services, which is fundamental to managers of public sport and leisure services.

This approach to performance management is flexible in that the process of deciding what should be the focus of the scorecard should allow managers to clarify the strategy of the service. However, like all management techniques, problems can arise in the implementation of the Balanced Scorecard. First, there may be a problem with conflicting measures. Some measures, such as increases in online access in libraries and cost reduction, naturally conflict. The balance that will achieve the best results must be determined after consideration of the service's objectives. Second, as discussed in Chapter 4, in the public sport and leisure sector there is the difficulty of selecting performance indicators to measure social objectives. Third, performance measurement is only useful if it initiates appropriate management action. There is little point in developing a set of measures for the four aspects of the scorecard, if managers are not going to react to the information that these generate or cannot control the outcome. Finally, managers need to have the skills to be able to interpret the information that the Balanced Scorecard generates.

There are many other performance management frameworks that can be adopted. In order to support these, there are three factors that are integral to successful performance management. First, it is important for the organisation to have a culture that supports performance management. An effective performance management framework is more than just a system of controlling the operations of an organisation; it must also encourage staff to consider performance management as a fundamental way of doing things. As outlined above, staff are the key to making sure that procedures and operations actually meet targets and thus, the organisation's culture has to support this process.

Second, the organisation must be clear about its purpose and priorities, as this will determine what has to be achieved and what has to be achieved first. Organisational purpose and priorities will dictate what services should achieve, as service plans should be developed to contribute to overall objectives. Without organisational objectives, there is a danger that services pursue their own objectives, which may be in opposition to that required of the organisation. For example, in the 1990s, as a consequence of government legislation, some managers prioritised revenue over social objectives, despite all local authorities having key social objectives. An example of the purpose for parks and open spaces is presented in Figure 7.2.

Finally, in order to be effective, performance management systems must involve effective performance measurement and target setting. This is perhaps the key to making performance management effective, because if measures of performance are not established, then managers are not in a position to assess how they are doing, nor to be able to take corrective action if required. In addition, it is important to set levels of performance, or targets that are to be achieved, as this aids comparison with other organisations and with previous performance.

Performance management assists in four main ways. First, and somewhat obviously, performance management assists with planning as it provides a structure for controlling the implementation of plans to meet objectives, provides information on how the service is performing against targets and generates information that can be fed into future planning. Indeed, without performance management, planning is a pointless process. Second, and closely associated with this is that performance management allows managers to evaluate the success of the service in achieving strategies and in implementing policy. Third, performance management improves operational

---

To contribute to the quality of life of residents and others through:

- ensuring that all residents and visitors are aware of park and open space amenities;
- ensuring access of residents and visitors to parks and open spaces;
- organising events and consider targeting of specials needs groups;
- ensuring that the standards of maintenance of parks and open spaces are adequate;
- ensuring that the service provided is cost-effective.

Figure 7.2 The purpose of parks and open spaces.

Source: Howell and Badmin, 1996.

ownership and does this in two ways. Managers who are aware of the organ-isation as a whole and of how their service is performing are in a strong position to influence decision making in the organisation. Knowledge of performance and the ability to manage it increases the expert power of public sport and leisure professionals. In addition, ownership is increased when staff know how their job is contributing to organisational objectives and how their service is performing in comparison with others. Performance manage-ment allows this and promotes the culture of new managerialism discussed in Chapter 2. The final benefit of performance management is that it allows managers to focus on key aspects of the service, such as quality or equity. The information produced from performance management allows managers to evaluate how they are doing against objectives set in targeted areas.

Barriers to performance management

Although there are clearly benefits to performance management, there are also barriers to its effectiveness. First, managers must accept the need for performance management and use it as a key management tool. If a manager's attitude to performance management is negative, it will not be used effectively within the management of the service. Second, there needs to be a performance management structure in place in the organisation, which incorporates the setting of objectives, the procedures for the collec-tion and analysis of information and for comparison with targets. The lack of such a process will be a barrier. Third, using these techniques requires certain skills and without these performance management will not be effective. Indeed, without a clear understanding of the process involved and what the components mean, there is a danger that mistakes may occur in decision making, resulting in the service performing poorly. Finally, performance management suffers from areas of the service where there are poorly defined performance indicators. As will be discussed below, the social objectives of public provision make it difficult to define performance indicators for all operations. This makes it difficult to manage the performance of a significant part of the public sport and leisure service.

   Despite Best Value promoting performance management, the Audit Commission (2002: p. 14) noted that many providers needed to improve their performance management systems. In their inspection of these ser-vices inspectors found a number of common weakness. There were:

- no robust performance framework, or a system that is in its infancy and is not yet well understood or applied;
- too many or too few performance indicators that fail to measure key outcomes or do not enable the whole service to be appraised (for example, the use of financial indicators only, or facility PIs only);
- no use of wider PIs that could be used to measure personal leisure activity such as cycling, yoga or jogging;

- inconsistent, imprecise or ambiguous definitions of what data actually means; for example, an inability to distinguish the number of users from the number of visitors or relate financial performance to the achievement of outcomes such as increased participation levels;
- lack of robust baseline data and no trend analysis, which means little or no capacity to measure or analyse performance over time. There is also a lack of overall analysis of performance information across the whole service to identify areas of good and poor performance across all service areas, as well as specific aspects of the service;
- limited monitoring of whether service objectives are being achieved, often due to lack of targets or inappropriate and immeasurable performance measures being selected. This makes close scrutiny by members difficult.
- little or no analysis of existing customers and management information to match provision to the needs of different communities;
- limited use of PIs to measure the performance of contracted organisations or other partners who may be delivering key services on behalf of the authority;
- lack of comparison of performance, either across services or with other authorities or partners.

These are clearly major weaknesses that suggest that the performance management frameworks used by sport and leisure providers are taking some time to become effective. Indeed, the Audit Commission's (2002) reported the inadequate use of performance data and inadequate evaluation strategies. In addition, they noted that the data that was collected was often not used to inform management action.

Performance measurement

In order to evaluate performance it needs to be measured and all possible aspects of operations should be evaluated in order to inform management practice. Within sport and leisure services, performance measurement is usually carried out through the use of performance indicators. In order to make PIs more useful for management, they are usually associated with a target or level that managers need to obtain. Performance indicators perform several roles in the management of services. Performance indicators:

- clarify the organisation's objectives;
- evaluate the final outcome resulting from the organisation's activities;
- enable citizens to be informed about performance;
- enable citizens to make informed choices about their services;
- indicate the contribution of the service towards the organisation's objectives;

- act as a trigger for the further investigation of and possible action to improve the quality of inputs and outputs;
- assist with managerial decision making when allocating resources;
- provide staff with feedback to enable them to develop and improve operations.

(Holloway, 1999)

There are six key principles that underlie effective performance management (Audit Commission, 2000). First, it is important to be clear about the purpose of performance indicators. Managers must know who will be using the information and for what purpose. Customers, politicians, the general public and other managers will all require performance management information and this needs to be provided in a manner that is accessible and appropriate to their needs. For example, service users will want to know what service standards to expect and how the service is performing, while managers will want to monitor efficiency and effectiveness. These differing purposes are likely to require different PIs and will certainly require different presentations of the data.

Second, performance indicators are only effective if organisations are clear about the focus of their service and its priorities. This will allow objectives and activities that are important to the organisation to be identified and the criteria to measure these to be established. There are two main problems with this: first, what has to be achieved, the objectives of the service, may not be clear; and second, objectives that exist may not be clearly expressed in terms that lend themselves to measurement. This is primarily an issue to do with social objectives, although Best Value does require providers to attempt to express what they intend to achieve socially.

Third, performance measurement should be aligned with the objective setting and performance review process. There must be links between the PIs used for operational purposes and those that monitor corporate performance. The performance measurement system should have a hierarchy of measures, much the same as the planning system has a hierarchy of objectives. The measures that guide the performance of the service should contribute to those that guide the organisation as a whole.

Fourth, as outlined in the discussion of the Balanced Scorecard, the overall set of performance indicators should give a balanced picture of the organisation's performance. The PIs chosen should reflect the main aspects of the organisation, including outcomes and the perspectives of users. The Audit Commission (2000) has suggested that a balanced set of indicators should cover the following:

- economy, efficiency, effectiveness and outcome indicators;
- a mix of financial and non-financial data;
- measures of cost, time and quality;
- indicators that address the best value themes: strategy, cost-efficiency, outcomes, quality and fair access.

Fifth, performance indicators must be kept up to date to meet changing circumstances. This will require a balance between having consistent information to compare performance over time and taking advantage of improved data and changing local priorities.

Finally, performance indicators must be robust. The PIs selected must stand up to use over time. In order to make comparison meaningful, PIs need to be able to be collected in the same manner, from the same data, to measure the same operation. They must:

- be relevant to the aims and objectives of the organisation;
- be clearly defined to ensure consistent collection;
- be easy to understand and use;
- be comparable, and sufficiently accurate to allow comparisons between organisations and over time;
- be verifiable by senior managers, auditors and inspectors;
- be statistically valid, so that false conclusions are not made;
- be cost-effective to collect, so that the benefits of using the information outweigh the cost of collection;
- be unambiguous, so that it is clear what constitutes good performance;
- be attributable, so that the responsibility for achieving good performance is clear;
- be responsive, to reflect changes in performance clearly;
- avoid perverse incentives and the risk of skewing outcomes, and encourage behaviours leading to service improvement;
- allow innovation in service delivery;
- be timely, so that the information is not out of date.

(Audit Commission, 2000: p. 11)

Using performance indicators

There are a number of factors that need to be considered when using performance indicators in order to ensure that they are valuable in performance management (Howell and Badmin, 1996). First, the data on which PIs are based must be trusted, particularly if the data is being used for external comparison. The data used to form PIs must be collected from the same sources, in the same manner, in a rigorous fashion. This is essential so that managers can be certain that the performance that is being reported is accurate. Second, PIs must measure what they are considered to measure, otherwise they may lead to mistakes in management decision making. For example, counting the number of people who come through the door of a facility is often not a true indication of the number of users as this will include spectators who do not use the facilities. Third, it is important that PIs are only used as a guide for management, as they do not provide an explanation for performance. PIs will indicate areas of strengths and weakness, but will not say *why* these are strengths and weaknesses. This means that the interpretation of PIs is the key to performance management, rather than simply their measurement.

Performance indicators, on their own, are meaningless. Managers need to use them to review performance in the context of the inputs that were made, in comparison with objectives and in consideration of the whole collection of performance indicators. For example, a sport and leisure facility may be very effective in recouping its costs by having high fees to use the facility, but have done this at the expense of users on low incomes. In this case, the manager has been effective financially, but ineffective from the point of providing sport for all. Actual evaluation of performance has to be done in the context of what the facility was trying to achieve. If the local authority wanted the facility to recoup costs, the performance of the facility has been effective.

The Audit Commission (2000) has outlined a number of factors that makes the use of performance indictors more valuable to public managers. First, managers should only report on relevant information. It is suggested that managers limit the number of PIs that they use to between 10 and 20, so that actual performance is not hidden in an overwhelming amount of information. In addition, these indicators should be hierarchical, so that it is clear what is of key importance. Second, performance indicators should focus on actions. Performance management systems often generate information that is 'nice to know', but not overly helpful in managing or explaining performance. This information distracts from performance issues and should not be collected at the expense of meaningful data.

Third, the data must be used. Managers must demonstrate the value of PIs by using them in policy reviews, service evaluations and when giving constructive feedback to staff involved in the delivery of the service. Fourth, once a coherent package of PIs has been established, these need to be associated with targets in order to guide performance. Targets challenge the organisation to do better and will set standards of service for customers and citizens. Fifth, staff must see the value of performance indicators and use them to guide their performance. They should understand the link between the PIs used for their job and the PIs used to evaluate the organisation.

Sixth, there needs to be a balance between short- and long-term objectives. Pressure for immediate good performance can lead to attention being focused on short-term targets at the expense of long-term objectives. Seventh, the manipulation of data must be avoided. Performance indicators are only useful if they measure what is actually happening, rather than being used to present a desired picture of performance. A robust collection system and the clear definition of PIs will prevent this. Eighth, managers must measure what is important, not make important what can be measured. They must avoid measuring aspects of performance that are easy to measure, such as finance, and instead identify measures for those things that are important, such as social objectives. Finally, as suggested above, the information must be interpreted thoughtfully and accurately. Indicators do not provide the answer for why performance has occurred; the interpretation of indicators performs this task.

Comparison

The main purpose of performance measurement is comparison; that is, comparison with existing targets, with previous performance or with external organisations. The use of performance indicators to compare with previous performance has long been established within parts of the public sport and leisure service. External comparison of performance has been promoted by the introduction of Best Value and is occurring in these services in three ways. First, there is a requirement to use the Audit Commission Performance Indicators for Cultural Services, as outlined in Table 7.1, to compare performance with other local authorities. This national level of comparison is statutory and managers must collect data to allow these indictors to be established.

There have been a number of criticisms of the national PIs, despite the thorough consultation process that the Audit Commission has been through in order to devise them. Very few of the national indicators focus on effectiveness and there is an emphasis on economy and efficiency. Also, as mentioned above, performance indicators are not an explanation of performance. They do not say why an organisation has performed at a certain level, or assist those that perform poorly to improve their performance. Finally, the national performance indicators take no account of location, service priorities or catchment population. As a result, the national indicators do not present an explanatory picture of performance.

In an attempt to overcome this, managers have 'local' indicators that are specific to their local context allowing them to take account of relevant

Table 7.1 National performance indicators for cultural and leisure services

Strategic objective	Number of pupils visiting museums and galleries in organised school groups Does the local authority have a local cultural strategy?
Cost/efficiency	The cost per visit to public libraries Spend per head of population on cultural and recreational facilities
Service delivery outcome	The number of visits per head of population to public libraries
Quality	The percentage of library users who found the book(s) they wanted and/or the information they needed
Fair access	Percentage of residents by targeted group satisfied with the authority's cultural and recreational activities

Source: www.local_regions.odpm.gov.uk, 2002.

geographical, policy or catchment area characteristics. In addition, they compare themselves with services that are similar, in a 'like-with-like' comparison. For example, a small sports hall may compare itself with other small sports halls; urban parks can be compared with other urban parks. This type of comparison makes more sense than national comparison because the comparator is more appropriate and this like-with-like comparison is integral to the Sport England performance indicators for sports halls and swimming pools (Taylor *et al.*, 2000). These provide several points of comparison for managers of these facilities. Managers of sports halls and swimming pools can compare themselves with others on the basis of:

- the type of facility;
- facility size;
- catchment population characteristics.

The performance indicators chosen by Sport England fall into three groups:

- access: representing the extent to which facilities are used by different groups of users, particularly disadvantaged groups and new users;
- financial: representing subsidy, expenditure and income performance;
- utilisation: representing the scale and nature of the use and non-use of facilities.

The indicators also provide targets for managers of these facilities to compare themselves against, which assists with improving the performance of sports halls and swimming pools.

The third method of comparison is known as 'process comparison' or process benchmarking, which is often carried out through the use of the Quest framework (to be discussed in the next chapter). This occurs when managers compare organisational operations in order to learn from others. This type of comparison or benchmarking was referred to in Chapter 6; it occurs when managers identify functions or services that are also part of external organisations that they wish to compare their performance against. This is usually done with the purpose of learning from the external organisation in order to improve performance. For example, Taunton Deane Borough Council identified that it performed poorly in the area of staff absence through illness. The benchmarking project leader identified a local authority that was performing well in this area and investigated the processes used by this authority to control staff absence. This led to the introduction of new procedures and paperwork to manage the problem in Taunton Deane.

The process of comparing operations is valuable, as detailed information on how to improve can be obtained from the organisations being compared against. In addition, it allows managers to identify organisations outside the industry to act as comparators. For example, Taunton Deane Borough Council had identified a need to improve the induction process for new staff entering its sport and leisure service. After a thorough investigation of potential partners, a commercial restaurant was considered to be appropriate as it dealt with similar types of staff and staffing structures and had high staff turnover, a feature of the public sport and leisure industry. If it is a process that is being benchmarked, the business of the object of comparison becomes less important than its levels of performance.

Is performance management appropriate for public sport and leisure services?

Although performance management is integral to Best Value and Comprehensive Performance Assessment, there has been some debate about its appropriateness for the management of public services. Most of this concern has been focused on the role of performance indicators and Sanderson (1998) presented several concerns regarding the use of performance indicators in public services. First, he is unconvinced that performance indicators can deal with all aspects of the complex public sector environment. Performance indicators have existed for some time in areas such as finance, customer satisfaction and operations. However, they are yet to be fully developed to measure the contribution of a service to the health of the community or its ability to reduce crime. Sanderson (1998) feels that this will lead managers to focus on those aspects of the service that can be measured, rather than working to develop indicators for the aspects of the service that should be delivered. This is a valid point and his concern is borne out by the Audit Commission indicators that are outlined in Table 7.1, which focus on easily measurable aspects of the cultural and leisure services.

Second, he argues that performance management and measurement is based upon a fundamental assumption of *measurability*. The underlying premise of performance management is that all aspects of management can be measured. This assumption is clearly flawed, in that although it is possible to measure many aspects of public sport and leisure management, there are some factors that cannot be evaluated. For example, it is not possible to allocate a measure to the strength of the political process within a local authority. For some issues, politicians may let sport and leisure managers do as they see best, while for others politicians may demand that their recommendations are implemented. It is not possible to give this factor a weighting to incorporate it into decision making or to use it when making comparisons against other local authorities. There are many other aspects of public sport and leisure management that are difficult to measure, such as those already outlined that relate to social objectives, or factors such as changing customer tastes.

Third, and perhaps more importantly, performance management is based on the assumption of *controllability*. Performance management is based on the belief that all aspects of the service are under the control of managers. Sanderson (1998) argues that this assumption is also flawed, as managers have no control over changes in customer tastes, redundancies in the catchment area that lead to declining customer numbers or cuts in budget instigated by central government, politicians or other funding bodies.

Sanderson (1998: p. 13) has argued that the consequence of these three weaknesses in performance management and performance measurement is what he calls a 'potential for distorted focus and action'. The measurement of public sector performance is statutory as a result of Best Value and Sanderson (1998) argues that this will encourage managers to focus on the aspects that can be measured and to ignore those aspects that cannot. He suggests that this will lead to measures of economy and efficiency to be prominent at the cost of measures of effectiveness. It also means that financial and operational objectives are likely to be achieved, once again at the expense of social objectives. Thus, the performance management process will distort managerial focus away from social issues to operational issues.

It is difficult to argue strongly against the issues outlined above, as evidence can be found to support Sanderson's (1998) concerns. The national performance indicators for cultural and leisure services do not deal with social issues. The cost and quality focus of CCT led to a reduction in concern for social objectives, as these could not be written clearly into CCT contacts (Robinson, 1999a). There have, however, been attempts to overcome these weaknesses. The Sport England indicators include access indicators for socially excluded groups. The Best Value audit process (Audit Commission, 2002) presents evidence of sport and leisure services that have addressed social issues and have service objectives and plans that relate to issues of social exclusion. However, the main way of dealing with Sanderson's (1998) concerns will be in the way that PIs are interpreted and presented to stakeholders for their review. Local performance plans allow managers to put performance in the context of local priorities for the service and thus will overcome some of the weaknesses of the national comparison. As long as a balanced set of PIs are collected and are interpreted in a contextual manner, then performance management is an appropriate tool for the management of public sport and leisure services.

Summary and conclusions

This chapter has considered the role of performance management in the delivery of public sport and leisure services, outlining the major issues that affect the management of performance in these services. Despite the Best Value legislation promoting performance management, there is evidence to suggest that this is not fully integrated into these services. As a result, the Audit Commission has published a number of resources to assist with this.

In addition, there have been concerns expressed about the viability of managing the performance of public services as a result of the need to establish social objectives, reflect political priorities and account for citizen's preferences. The main solution to these concerns is in the interpretation of the performance indicators collected. Managers must use indicators to explain performance as the factors outlined above will impact on how services are able to perform. All of this makes the management of the performance of public sport and leisure organisations more complex and challenging than that of commercial organisations.

Suggested tasks for further study

• Develop a balanced set of objectives and PIs for a sport and leisure service of your choice.
• Develop PIs that measure the contribution that sport and leisure makes to decreases in crime. Make a note of the issues involved.
• Identify suitable benchmarking partners for handling telephone bookings in a public sport and leisure service. Make a note of why this organisation may be suitable.

Further reading

Howell, S. and Badmin, P. (1996) *Performance, Monitoring and Evaluation in Leisure Management*, London: Pitman Publishing.

8   Quality management

This chapter aims to discuss the phenomenon of quality management and its role in the public sport and leisure industry. It provides a brief history of the development of the quality movement and considers the appropriateness of the concept within the current public context. The chapter also considers the relevance of prominent definitions of quality and outlines a framework for the management of service quality. Within this, it evaluates the merits of the main quality programmes available to managers. Finally, it discusses whether quality management is appropriate for public sport and leisure services.

The emergence of quality management within the public sector

In 1980, a programme called *If Japan Can, Why Can't We?* was broadcast in America. During the programme it became apparent that an American, W. Edwards Deming, had been responsible for the culture of management that had transformed the struggling Japanese economy to one that was synonymous with quality. Through a series of lectures on quality control and management responsibility, Deming advocated a philosophy or vision of a 'constancy of purpose' that resulted in the movement away from quality inspection to a management culture encouraging quality in all of its operations.

Deming's work in Japan was continued by Joseph Juran who emphasised the role of communication, management and people in the pursuit of quality. In doing so he was responsible for bringing together a number of unconnected quality approaches to formulate an integrated management philosophy. The quality movement gained worldwide momentum through the further work of people such as Philip Crosby, John Oakland and Tom Peters, eventually spreading to all sectors of industry. Table 8.1 outlines the key principles of quality management advocated by these quality gurus.

Concern with quality as a management concept was a phenomenon of the 1990s, emerging as managers sought to respond to the changes in their

Table 8.1 Gurus of quality management

Characteristics	Deming	Juran	Feigenbaum	Crosby	Peters
Definition of quality	Predictable degree of uniformity and dependability at low cost	Fitness for purpose	Total quality control throughout the organisation	Conformance to requirements	Customers' perception of excellence
General approach	Reduce variability, continuous improvement	Emphasis on management of human aspects	Application of quality systems throughout the organisation	Prevention of errors	Total customer responsiveness
Judges of quality	Users	Benefits to users	Customers	Meeting of set standards	Customers
Structure to managing quality	14 points	10 steps	10 benchmarks	14 steps – 5 absolutes	7 patterns
Senior management responsibility	Responsible for 94% of problems	Responsible for more than 80% of problems	Leadership, but with a quality manager	Responsible for quality	Should be passionate about quality
Teamwork	Employee participation in decisions	Team/quality circle approach	Individual and teamwork zealotry, quality circles	Quality improvement teams; quality councils	Cross-functional teams
Performance standard	Many scales, use statistical process charts	Meets required purpose	Continuous upwards moving targets	Zero defects; setting performance indicators	Measure everything
Basis for improvement	Continuous: eliminate goals	Project-based approach: set goals	Continuous improvement to have total customer satisfaction	A process, not a programme	Create a shadow quality organisation in parallel

Source: Adapted from Williams and Buswell, 2003.

operating context that were presented and discussed in Chapter 2. Traditionally associated with levels of standard (i.e. low quality, high quality), the contemporary management use of the term 'quality' has evolved to indicate a good or excellent service. The quality gurus, mentioned above have argued that the principles of quality management are the way forward to ensure organisational success.

The emergence of quality management within UK public sport and leisure as an industry-wide concept first became evident in the early 1990s and became apparent as a result of two main features. First, the concept of 'customer care' (concern with customer satisfaction), which began in the late 1980s, became increasingly important to managers, indicated by the increasing prevalence of quality management within journals, as a focus for training courses and, perhaps more tellingly, within product advertising. Second, and in parallel, was the increasing use of the British Standards Institute's accredited quality programme BS5750 – the forerunner to the contemporary ISO9002 – which will be discussed later.

Throughout the 1990s the concern with quality expanded to incorporate the use of a wide variety of quality management methods, initiated the publication of a number of articles and books on quality management and eventually led to the industry-wide adoption of the vocabulary associated with quality management. In addition, quality and its management became important to the industry's professional bodies, ILAM and ISRM, and as indicated by the commissioning of articles and research and the themes of industry conferences. Most significantly, however, belief in the value of quality to the management of the UK leisure industry led to the development of Quest, a sport- and leisure-specific quality programme (see below) endorsed and promoted by the professional bodies previously mentioned, by leisure quangos such as Sport England, and by other interested parties.

The vocabulary of quality management

The general acceptance of the word quality into 'management-speak' has not, however, led to a generally accepted definition of what is meant by quality. As a result, a variety of definitions of quality have been promoted by the proponents of quality management. For example, the definition offered by Deming (1986) focuses on the need to *exceed* customer expectations which emphasises the role of the customer in the delivery process; Juran (1988) emphasises conformance to requirements; while the definition of the British Standards Institute (1987: p. 1) refers to the need to consider the characteristics that make up the service to be delivered by defining quality as 'the totality of features and characteristics of a product or service that bear on its ability to satisfy a given need'.

It is, however, the definition of Clarke (1992: p. 23) that is considered to be an appropriate definition of quality for the public sport and leisure industry and he defines quality as 'how consistently the product or service delivered, meets or exceeds the customers' expectations and needs'. The strength of this definition is that first, there is awareness that *meeting* expectations can provide an acceptable level of quality. Second, both expectations and needs must be addressed. Finally, there must be a consistency of delivery, which is a key criterion for the assessment of service quality.

The main weakness of the above definitions is their tendency to become forgotten slogans, which led Gaster (1995) to suggest that a generic definition of quality for public services may be inappropriate. Instead, it is more important to define quality in terms that are meaningful to individual organisations. This is because staff are more likely to be committed to a definition of quality that is directly related to the operations of their service. In addition, the organisation's definition of quality will highlight what is important when aiming to deliver a quality service. Quality therefore needs to be defined in terms that are directly relevant to the organisation.

For example, in one local authority quality is defined as 'producing standards of service in our facilities which mean that customers will be encouraged to return to use our facilities'. For this local authority, quality was used as a technique for retaining customers and as a result, management activities were all geared to meeting the 'standards of service' referred to above. Another local authority defined quality in a similar manner, for a similar purpose, as 'providing certain standards which the customer will appreciate which means that they will make repeat visits'.

In a third local authority, quality is defined as 'the best possible service at the lowest cost'. For this authority and others, quality has to be delivered within budget constraints indicating a strong awareness of the financial difficulties affecting public sport and leisure services management.

Having defined quality it is useful to identify the three other commonly used terms of quality management. These are quality control, quality assurance and quality programmes. Quality control has been defined by the British Standards Institute (1987: p. 1) as 'the operational techniques and activities that are used to fulfil requirements for quality', which in sport and leisure terms encompasses such activities as testing chlorine levels and inspection of equipment and toilets for cleanliness.

One stage further in the quality process is quality assurance which is 'all of those planned and systematic actions necessary to provide confidence that a product or service will satisfy given requirements for quality' (British Standards Institute, 1987: p. 1). This incorporates organisational processes such as staff training and development, but also mechanical items such as thermostats on heating systems. The 'confidence' brought about by quality assurance decreases the need to check for errors as 'quality' is built in to the service delivery by the use of quality programmes. These can be described as a combination of working practices and appropriate procedures that ensure that the provision of quality is 'built in' to the organisation's activity.

Frameworks for managing quality

There are a variety of tools and techniques that are available to assist managers with the delivery of services of a high quality, which will be discussed in the remainder of this chapter. The following section outlines three frameworks for managing quality that allow a structured approach to quality management by focusing on all parts of the operation. All of these frameworks have a role to play in assisting managers to meet the requirements of Best Value as they emphasise performance management and continuous improvement. The first to be discussed is Total Quality Management (TQM), which develops an organisational culture of quality. This is followed by an outline of the European Foundation for Quality Management (EFQM) Excellence Model and then Quest, a leisure-specific quality framework.

Total Quality Management

Total Quality Management is a framework for quality management that aims to develop an organisational culture that has quality as its focus. It is a management philosophy, incorporating the following principles:

- a *customer orientation*, both internal and external, throughout the organisation;
- *clear and appropriate* organisational objectives;
- the *commitment and involvement of all staff*, led from the top of the organisation;
- a commitment to *seek to improve continuously* the operations of the organisation;
- the use of *systems and procedures* to assure quality;
- the regular *monitoring, measurement and feedback* of all operations;
- the *education and training* of all staff to ensure that they have the necessary knowledge and skills for the quality philosophy.

Those that support a TQM approach to management have advocated this framework as the way of guaranteeing success for organisations facing competition. This is because organisations that use a TQM approach to managing quality have to set clear organisational goals and establish standards of service. More importantly, TQM is based on the concept of continuous improvement and organisations that use this framework to manage quality need to be customer focused and innovative.

The philosophy inherent in TQM is to be lauded and it can be argued that TQM should be the goal of all public sport and leisure services managers. There are, however, some weaknesses to the TQM framework. Although these are discussed in detail by Robinson (1997), the first area of weakness is the need to be completely customer-focused by identifying and meeting the needs of all customer groups. Given the large number of groups who can claim to be customers of local authority sport and leisure services, this will present problems. Another barrier to achieving TQM will be the development of clearly expressed objectives, including social objectives and the use of appropriate performance indicators that measure all aspects of the service. Finally, the political culture of public sport and leisure services may inhibit the development of a true culture of quality, which is intrinsic to the success of Total Quality Management.

EFQM Excellence Model

This framework for managing quality was introduced at the beginning of 1992 and has become the most widely used organisational framework in Europe. It is a non-prescriptive framework that recognises that there are many different approaches to reaching and sustaining excellence. The principles of the EFQM Excellence Model are:

* *results orientation*: excellence is dependent on balancing and satisfying the needs of all relevant stakeholders;
* *customer focus*: the customer is the final arbiter of quality and this needs to be optimised through a clear focus on the need of current and potential customers;
* *leadership and constancy of purpose*: leaders create clarity and unity of purpose;
* *management by process and facts*: organisations perform more effectively when all activities are understood and systemically managed by decisions based on reliable information;
* *people development and involvement*: the full potential of staff is released through shared values, a culture of trust and empowerment;
* *continuous learning, innovation and improvement*: performance is maximised when it is based on the sharing of knowledge and a culture of continuous learning;
* *partnership development*: an organisation works more effectively when it has mutually beneficial relationships with its partners that are built on trust;
* *public responsibility*: organisations must adopt an ethical approach and exceed the expectations and regulations of the community at large.

This model is a practical tool to help organisations structure their approach to quality management and the EFQM model is becoming increasingly popular in the management of public sport and leisure services. This is primarily because it is the underpinning model for delivering quality services in the Best Value legislation and was the basis of Quest.

For further information on EFQM go to www.efqm.org

Quest

Quest is a sport- and leisure-specific quality framework which aims to set industry standards for quality and good practice within a customer-focused management framework, by encouraging managers of sport and leisure facilities to consider their operations from the customer's point of view. Launched in September 1996, Quest has been supported and promoted by a wide range of organisations, such as the four home country Sports Councils, the Local Government Association, ISRM, ILAM and the Fitness Industry Association, who have endorsed and financed the drive for the initiative. There is a Quest scheme for facility management and for sport development.

The Quest scheme for facility management identifies 22 critical management issues that are grouped into the following four areas:

- facilities operation;
- customer relations;
- staffing;
- service development and improvement.

A key strength of this programme is that it requires managers to address all aspects of their operations and customer satisfaction.

The assessment process for Quest includes three main stages. First, managers are required to carry out a self-assessment phase when they compare the operations of their organisation against the assessment criteria for the award. This indicates areas of strength and areas for improvement. For many managers, this process itself is enough to improve the quality of service; however, for those who wish to seek external recognition the next process is two assessment visits. These are carried out by trained assessors and one visit is a mystery customer visit when an assessor visits the facility to use it in the guise of a customer.

Facility managers feel that the main benefit of Quest is its potential for reviewing procedures and getting feedback on these (Robinson and Crowhurst 2001). As a result, the self-assessment aspect of the quality framework is considered to be vitally important. In addition, Quest is felt to be a useful tool for benchmarking the industry as it is the only industry-specific quality framework.

For more information on Quest go to www.sportengland.org

Issues in managing quality

A customer focus

In order to deliver public sport and leisure services that are perceived to be of a high quality, managers must know who their main customer groups are and then focus the service on these customers. This is because services must be delivered to meet the requirements and expectations of these customers (Robinson and Wolsey, 1996; Meyer and Blümelhuber, 1998) and without the identification of these needs, there is a danger that the delivery of high-quality services will happen by chance, rather than being managed.

All sport and leisure organisations have more than one customer group and managers of public sector organisations have four customer groups:

- paying customers, such as those who use the service or pay for others to use the service;
- internal customers, such as staff and other departments;
- politicians, such as local councillors or the Minister for Sport;
- citizens, such as those who pay council tax.

In addition, within each of these customer groups, there are further segments based on characteristics identified by the organisation as being important. For example, paying customers are traditionally divided into sub-groups on the basis of demographic variables such as age and life cycle. This greatly increases the number of customer groups that public sport and leisure organisations have and means that meeting the requirements and expectations of all customers is virtually impossible due to resource limitations and conflicting requirements. In order to manage service quality successfully, it is therefore necessary for managers to prioritise their customer groups. If customers are not prioritised, then managers will find it difficult to decide where to focus quality management activities and run the risk of delivering services that do not meet any expectations of quality.

The criteria used to prioritise customer groups should be linked to the objectives of the organisation, so for public sport and leisure services, customers who generate income will be important as revenue is needed to reduce the cost of providing these services. Of equal importance, however, will be customer groups who are the focus of social objectives relating to social inclusion. For example, people on low incomes should be as important as those who generate revenue by doing fitness activities. It is inevitable that there will be several groups who are considered to be important; however, these must be put into some priority order. It may be possible, through careful programming of service delivery, to meet the needs of many of these customers, or indeed to meet many of the needs of all of them. It is important, however, that a priority is established so that in times of resource constraint, managers know whose requirements and expectations need to be met.

Expectations of service quality

It is widely accepted that customers determine service quality by comparing actual performance of the service with what they expected of the service (Parasuraman *et al.*, 1988, 1994). As a result, an understanding of what customers expect from an organisation is crucial to the management of its service quality.

If the service delivered meets customers' expectations, then the service is meeting customers' standards of service quality. If the service exceeds expectations, then the customers are 'delighted' and perceive service quality to be good. Alternatively, if the service does not meet expectations, service quality is perceived to be poor. Therefore managers need to, at a minimum, meet the expectations of their customers in order to deliver a service that is perceived to be of acceptable quality.

Customer expectations impact on service quality in two ways. First, knowledge of the attributes and features that customers expect from the service is essential as it allows managers to identify what must be provided in order to be considered to be providing an acceptable service. Second and perhaps more importantly, it is necessary to understand how important these attributes are to customers in order to ensure that they are delivered at a level that is acceptable (Meyer and Blümelhuber, 1998). Thus, knowledge of what customers expect and the level of expectation is paramount (Howat *et al.*, 1996; Parasuraman *et al.*, 1988, 1994; Robinson, 1999b).

It is generally agreed that service quality is made up of a variety of factors ranging from what is delivered, to how it is delivered and where it is delivered. From a programme of research with customers of public sport and leisure centres, Lentell (2000) established that the 18 attributes outlined in Table 8.2 were considered to be very important in the delivery of service quality.

These attributes must be present in public sport and leisure centres. In addition, they must be present at a standard that is considered to be acceptable to the priority customer groups. These standards have to be set in consultation with customers to ensure that acceptable levels of service quality are delivered. The role of consultation has been emphasised by Patmore and Tomes (1994: p. 4), who said:

> The dialogue with customers and stakeholders provides the information base which enables the organisation to review its service specifications, and to codify or recodify the ways in which it delivers services.

It is important, however, to be aware that the setting of standards should not be a one-off exercise. Walsh (1991) identified that as people become used to a service they begin to expect more. The current level of quality becomes the norm, forcing standards to change and align themselves with rising expectations, so the standards set six months earlier may no longer be perceived as providing high levels of quality. For example, if a facility supplies its customers with vending machines for refreshments, this is initially seen as adding value, and thus quality, to the service. Over time,

Table 8.2 Dimensions of service quality for public sport and leisure organisations

Dimensions	Attributes
Physical evidence	Centre cleanliness
	Centre maintenance
	Quality of equipment
	Maintenance of equipment
	Physical comfort
	Centre pleasant to be in
	Centre well run
	Centre well organised
Staff	Friendly
	Responsive
	Presentable
	Identifiable
	Experienced
	Knowledgeable
Secondary services	Timeliness of service and timekeeping
	Information
	Range of services
	Food and drink facilities

Source: Lentell, 2000.

however, this becomes an expectation and instead of valuing the machines, customers may begin to complain about limited choice, the lack of hot food and the cost of the machines. Managers have to respond to these complaints in order to meet expected standards of quality.

In addition to this, setting standards for the service does not overcome the fact that customers have different expectations of service quality. Meyer and Blümelhuber (1998: p. 59) have described quality as being a *relative* term saying:

> Two customers could receive the same services and may have two different opinions with respect to quality owing to different expectations, different selective perceptions and different dimensions of quality to which reference was made in order to assess the quality.

As a result, it is virtually impossible to set standards to ensure that all customers will have an experience that they perceive to be of good quality. What is important to one customer group may not be to another and indeed the provision of a high level of service to one group may detract from the service for another. For example, making a sports hall available for a basketball tournament will prevent other types of sport from being played in the facility. In addition, the standards of quality for the same service differ between customers. A child is likely to be less concerned with the safety of water slides and more concerned about the speed and the length of the slide. For parents these concerns tend to be reversed. This, once again, reinforces the value of prioritising customer groups, as managers can resolve these conflicts by referring to the expectations of the group that is considered to be the main priority.

Once standards for quality have been established, managers then need to put in place strategies for meeting the standards. For many managers this leads to the use of quality programmes, which are discussed below, as these assist in managing the parts of the service that can be specified, standardised and are primarily within management control.

Managing customer satisfaction

Once understood, customer expectations need to be managed and the main issue to be addressed is the measurement of satisfaction with existing services. Stabler (1996) has rightly argued that without measuring customer satisfaction it will be difficult to manage customer expectations because what customers expect dictates their level of satisfaction with the service. Unfortunately, customer satisfaction is never constant. As discussed earlier expectations of service standards increase over time, different people perceive the same service to have different levels of service quality and customer satisfaction with a service can be influenced by unrelated external factors such as work, traffic and weather condition.

Quality programmes and public sport and leisure facilities

The value of quality programmes in managing service quality is recognised by public sport and leisure managers and a significant number of local authorities have introduced quality programmes into the management of their services. Research carried out by Robinson and Crowhurst (2001) showed that nearly half of local authorities were using quality programmes in the management of their services and that most were using more than one programme. Table 8.3 shows the relative popularity of different programmes used in the management of public facilities and from this it is clear that Investors in People is the most commonly used programme.

Table 8.3 Quality programmes used in the management of public sport and leisure facilities

Programme	Number of local authorities	%
Investors in People	126	77
ISO9002	46	28
Charter Mark	29	18

Note
Number of authorities surveyed = 163.

The quality programmes outlined above and discussed below are developed and assessed by agencies who outline the procedures to be implemented and then assess the organisation to see if they follow these procedures. For example, the British Standards Institute developed, assesses and awards the programme ISO9002. These programmes are known as externally accredited programmes and achieving the award of these programmes is considered to be an indicator of service quality. As quality programmes have clearly defined objectives and require a full assessment of the aspect of the service that they focus on, they are useful in providing a structured means of focusing on the quality of the service. They have, however, a tendency to be inflexible, requiring adherence to a formatted structure and are relatively costly to gain and maintain. Table 8.4 outlines the characteristics of the main quality programmes.

Investors in People

Investors in People (IiP) is a human-resource-centred management initiative that aims to introduce quality management through the training and development of staff and the communication of business goals. Formally launched in 1991, IiP is supported by the Learning and Skills Councils and Business Link, who offer a range of services aimed at providing assistance, such as advisory visits, networking seminars and workshop events. Any organisation reaching the recognised standard in the following four criteria receives the investors award and is classified as an 'Investor in People'. This denotes:

- commitment from management to develop all employees in order to achieve business objectives;
- regular planning and review of organisational aims and objectives and what people need to do to achieve these;
- action to train and develop individuals on recruitment and throughout employment to improve performance;
- evaluation of the organisation's investment in training and development to assess achievement and to improve future effectiveness.

There are several advantages of IiP in an industry that relies on staff to deliver services of a high quality. Investors in People UK claim that the quality programme leads to improved earnings, improved productivity and profitability. More importantly, it leads to greater motivation of staff through involvement and personal development, a claim supported by the research of Robinson and Crowhurst (2001) who found that public sport and leisure providers felt that IiP increased staff involvement and morale. In addition, they found that IiP increased staff awareness of organisational objectives issues, which is a key objective of the programme.

From this, the role of IiP in managing service quality is evident.

Table 8.4 The characteristics of externally awarded quality programmes

Name	ISO9002	Investors in People	Charter Mark	Quest
Award/certification body	BSI and other registered bodies	Learning and Skills Councils	Charter Mark Administration Service	Industry Policy Committee
Length of awards	As long as the organisation complies with the standard	3 years	3 years	2 years
Eligibility	Any organisation	Any organisation	Public sector organisations and other organisations providing public services	Leisure organisations
Criteria for achievement of award	Must satisfy standard procedural requirements and have them running 3 months before application is assessed	Must satisfy 24 assessment indicators aimed at improving performance through development of staff	Ten criteria based on the principles of public service	Must meet minimum standards in 22 management criteria
Application process	Submission of a quality manual of procedures as required by the standard	Submission of an action plan which gives clear evidence of resources for training and developing employees	Written applications no longer than 13 pages and supporting information providing evidence that each criterion is reached	Organisation makes self assessment measured against criteria then applies for assessment
Cost of application	Approx. £1,500 for initial registration of an organisation, £1,000 every year following	No charge and there is often funding available from LSCs to assist application	Depends on number of staff and sites. Starts at £375	Minimum of £750 for initial assessment plus £600 to maintain registration
Judging process	Initial 3-day assessment visit and twice-yearly checks following accreditation	Assessment of written application and site visit to talk to employees	Panel assesses written application and visits all short-listed organisations	Mystery customer visit and assessment visit
Form of award/certification	Certificate, use of logo and trophy	Certificate, use of logo and plaque	Certificate, use of logo and trophy	Certificate and plaque

Although it is impossible to guarantee an appropriate response from staff, a good training and development programme, linked to the objectives of the organisation is likely to increase the quality of the customer–staff interaction by improving morale, ensuring knowledge and skills and increasing communication. As a result, IiP can make a significant contribution to the management of quality by improving staff responsiveness, competence and credibility.

The time and financial commitment required to resource Investors in People is a disadvantage for many organisations; however, it can be argued that employers should have these resources available as a matter of course as they relate to staff. It can also be argued that IiP is awarded to organisations that demonstrate little other than good practice in the management of people. In addition, there is some disadvantage to making Investors in People an achievement, in that organisations that are sceptical of the value of IiP may ignore the human resources aspects of their organisation.

For further information on IiP go to www.iip.co.uk

ISO9002

Originally developed by the British Standards Institute for manufacturing industry, ISO9002 sets out how an organisation should establish, document and maintain an effective quality management system. Based on a manual of defined operating procedures and standards of performance, the process to be followed in order to achieve registration of ISO9002 is relatively straightforward, but somewhat laborious.

All operations undertaken by the organisation must be identified and procedures need to be developed for ensuring the consistency of these. This means drawing up work instructions for staff who are carrying out these operations and setting associated standards. The manual must also outline a set of corrective actions for dealing with problems. Managers can carry this out simply as a self-assessment exercise, but may also seek accreditation to the ISO9002 standard. Accreditation is gained when the auditors have carried out a detailed check to ensure that the organisation successfully operates the quality system laid out in the manual. Once accredited, the systems must continue to be followed as there are regular inspections for as long as accreditation is maintained.

One obvious strength of this quality programme is that it requires organisations to identify all service operations, to write procedures for these operations and then to set associated performance standards. This is invaluable in managing the quality of the specified service and has a role to play in ensuring that operations such as staff training and satisfaction measurement are carried out. In addition, ISO9002 is extremely valuable as a tool for helping staff to know what they have to do in their work roles (Robinson and Crowhurst, 2001).

As a method of quality assurance, ISO9002 assists with the reliability of the leisure service by ensuring that the operations of the service are carried out in a consistent and standardised manner. Customers can expect the service to be consistent from day to day and between service deliverers within the local authority. The incorporation of staff training and development activities into the work instructions helps to ensure that staff are competent and accessible.

ISO9002 has an inherent weakness in that, although it requires the systems incorporated into the manual to meet set standards, the auditors do not necessarily evaluate these standards. Therefore it is possible to successfully obtain registration of ISO9002 without setting standards that guarantee a quality service, or indeed setting standards that are acceptable to customers. For example, if the manual states that ten inspection checks of equipment will be carried out, the organisation will be audited to see if it has done this – there is no assessment of whether anything was fixed as a result of the checks. If ISO9002 is not used properly, its award may not be an indication of quality.

For more information on ISO9002 go to www.emea.bsi-global.com

The Charter Mark

The Charter Mark is a major part of the government's drive to improve the quality of public services and has the objective of recognising and rewarding excellence in the delivery of public services. It is only available to public providers or those who provide services to the public. Contenders are required to submit a maximum of a 13-page report that outlines how they meet these ten criteria:

- standards: standards of service delivery must be set, monitored and published;
- information and openness: full and understandable information must be made available about the running of services, including information on costs and performance;
- consultation and involvement: providers must consult with users and potential users and staff and use their views to improve services;
- access and promote choice: services must be available to everyone who needs them and choice must be available where possible;
- fair treatment: all people must be treated fairly in a courteous and helpful manner;
- putting things right: services must have a complaints procedure leading to an apology, an explanation and a remedy;
- effective use of resources: services should be run in a manner that provides best value for taxpayers and users;
- innovation and improvement: providers must be able to demonstrate continuous improvements in services and facilities;

- co-ordination: local authorities must work with other providers to ensure that services are co-ordinated and effective;
- user satisfaction: providers need to be able to demonstrate user satisfaction.

The Charter Mark requires local authorities to address the desires of customers through consultation and to provide services that are convenient to users and to provide information in an understandable form. The Charter Mark has also forced public sport and leisure services to become more accountable to the public, by requiring the publishing of performance standards. It is inherently customer-oriented and also assists with the management of the characteristics of responsiveness and communication and voice.

The main weakness of the Charter Mark is the assessment and application process, as some managers felt that the 13-page application limited their ability to 'sell' their service (Robinson and Crowhurst, 2001). In addition, there were concerns that assessment of the award was carried out primarily without using the service or talking to customers.

For additional information on the Charter Mark go to www.chartermark.gov.uk.

Is quality management appropriate for public sport and leisure services?

Quality management is an integral part of the management of public sport and leisure services, as can be seen from Figure 8.1, which presents the quality strategy of King's Lynn and West Norfolk Borough Council.

It is important, however, to consider whether its use is actually appropriate for public services. Research evaluating the impact that quality management has had on UK public sport and leisure services suggests that the way that facility managers, in particular, have operationalised quality management makes it possible to argue that it is not appropriate for public sport and leisure services (Robinson, 2002).

As outlined above, public sport and leisure services have a wide variety of customer groups and the need to focus on key customer groups is considered fundamental to the provision of a quality service. Questions about the appropriateness of quality management arise from the groups that facility managers have identified as their priority customers. Research carried out by Robinson (1999a) showed a clear evidence of a focus on paying customers to the exclusion of other customer groups such as socially excluded members of the community. Without exception, Robinson (1999a) found that the customer who paid for the service was the focus of quality management activities. This was also found by Guest and Taylor (1999) who measured customer orientation in public sport and leisure services.

The Leisure and Tourism Department of the Borough of King's Lynn and West Norfolk provides a range of sports and tourism services to the residents of the borough and its visitors. This includes sports and cultural facilities, sports and arts development activities, tourism and grounds maintenance. The service employs 165 permanent staff.

The Department has a comprehensive approach to service quality, aimed at providing services of a standard that encourages people to return. To assist with this, the Department has been achieved accreditation of a number of quality programmes:

- 1992, 1995 and 1998: Investors in People;
- 1993, 1996 and 1999: Charter Mark;
- 1996: ISO9002 in sports facilities, which was extended in 1999 to cover seafront operations;
- 1999: Quest registration for three facilities; an additional facility has since achieved registration. Two of the facilities were rated in the top 8 per cent nationally.

In addition, the Department has had a number of awards:

- one of four commended finalists in the eastern Excellence Award of the British Quality Foundation;
- rated as 'Excellent, Probably Will Improve' by the Best Value Auditing Team.

The Auditing Team noted many features that have made King's Lynn and West Norfolk Borough Council a provider of top-quality public sport and leisure services. The Department offers a number of projects that cater to a wide range of needs. There are programmes of preventative maintenance and there is provision for the replacement of equipment. The Department responds to information from users, building their feedback into programme and service delivery. As a consequence, an average of 86 per cent of customers rated the arts service as 'good' or 'excellent' value for money, 80 per cent gave the same rating to the sport and leisure facilities. The Tourism Service was rated 'good' or 'excellent' by 85 per cent of customers.

Figure 8.1 Quality management in King's Lynn and West Norfolk Borough Council.

Source: www.westnorfolk.gov.uk

If local authorities only consider paying customers in the delivery of their services, it is possible to argue that quality management may undermine the rationale for the public subsidy of public sport and leisure that was outlined in Chapter 1. The key reason why such facilities have continued to be provided by the state is to ensure access for all citizens to recreational opportunities through price subsidies and targeted programming. It is access and the rights of citizenship that have traditionally provided the continued justification for the subsidy of public facilities.

The focus on paying customers is perhaps not a fundamental issue for many public services, particularly social services, as customers are commonly drawn from the less advantaged sectors of the community and are arguably the individuals most in need of the service. As such, it could be argued that those not using the service do not need the service and therefore do not require consideration. This is, however, rarely the case with sport and leisure services and the focus on the paying customer may lead to the exclusion of needy groups, as non-users, rather than not needing or wanting the service, may face particular barriers to accessing it. Thus, without explicit attempts to overcome these barriers, quality management may undermine the traditional market failure rationale for the existence of public sport and leisure facilities. If this is the case, can quality management be considered appropriate for public sport and leisure services?

The solution to this problem is to consider these services as a whole. Although facilities provide a significant number of sport and leisure opportunities and account for a large part of the budget, other aspects of the service minimise the limitations of the paying customer-focused approach that appears prevalent in UK public sport and leisure management. Outreach, development and community services are focused on those members of communities who cannot or will not use facilities and thus go a long way to extending access to public sport and leisure services.

In addition, by working in partnership, facility managers and outreach workers can develop programming and pricing strategies that encourage use by less 'profitable' customers, thereby justifying the continued subsidy of facilities through increased community access. The presence of 'leisure card' schemes in public sport and leisure services provides evidence of this type of strategy. As a result, although there may be focus on paying customers in the management of facilities, social objectives remain important as they are the focus of other parts of the service.

Summary and conclusions

This chapter has considered the role of quality management in the delivery of public sport and leisure services, outlining the major issues that affect the management of quality. Despite some concerns about the appropriateness of quality management, it is apparent from the research presented in this chapter that quality management and its associated techniques are valuable management tools for sport and leisure managers. Indeed, research carried out by Robinson (1999b) suggests that quality management is the vital key to the successful management of public sport and leisure services, much as it is for the commercial sector.

Suggested tasks for further study

- Compare and evaluate the quality management strategies adopted by one commercial leisure organisation and one public sport and leisure organisation.
- Identify the role of quality management within the context of 'Best Value'.
- Evaluate the concept of the 'public service orientation' for public sport and leisure services.

Further reading

Williams, C. and Buswell, J. (2003) *Service Quality in Leisure and Tourism*, Wallingford: CABI.

9   The management of change

One of the few constant factors in the management of public sport and leisure services is the need to respond to continually changing operating environments. This requires 'things to be different' in that managers have to seek out and identify management practices, organisational procedures and services that need to be altered or changed in order to respond effectively to the factors in the operating environments. Once these have been identified, these changes need to be developed and then implemented into the organisation. By doing this managers are considered to be managing change and effective managers will recognise when change is desirable or inevitable and will respond accordingly.

This chapter aims to discuss the management of effective change within public sport and leisure organisations. It begins by considering approaches to understanding organisational change and then discusses the factors that ensure that change is successfully introduced into public sport and leisure services. It also considers the barriers to change within these services and ends with a discussion of the management approaches that can be used to introduce change.

Understanding change

In order to manage change, it is necessary to understand how change occurs in public sport and leisure organisations, as this allows managers to take account of the factors required to successfully introduce change. In addition, the introduction of change is sometimes unsuccessful or does not achieve the desired consequences and if managers are aware of how change has occurred they will be able to identify why.

There are three main approaches to understanding how change occurs within public sport and leisure organisations (Pettigrew *et al.*, 1992; Spurgeon and Barwell, 1991). The first of these is the rational approach to understanding change, which is based on the premise that change can be planned, implemented and assessed in a systematic and measured manner. Managers scan their external environment looking for factors that may require change (see Chapter 4), identify and test potential changes and implement these in a planned manner within the organisation.

Second is the structural approach to understanding change, which is based on the belief that the organisation's response to the external environment depends on its structure. For example, smaller organisations are considered to able to respond more rapidly to the environment and implement change more quickly. They may, however, lack the resources that would allow the most appropriate response to be introduced.

Finally, there is the contextual approach to change (Pettigrew, 1987), which considers that change can only be understood with an awareness of the process of interaction between people, the organisation's history, environmental context and the politics that operate. It is this final approach that is considered to be most appropriate for the understanding of change within public sport and leisure services, as change within these services rarely comes about as a result of a single factor in the external environment. Rather, as outlined in Chapter 2, it emerges as a result of the interactions between the operating context and the people within the organisation.

The contextualist approach to understanding change

In order to fully understand and explain organisational change and its implementation, it is necessary to understand all of the processes and issues that may have influenced the decision to implement change. Thus, analysis of organisational change must take account of the organisational environments, the type of change under consideration and the process of the development of the change programme. In an attempt to explain this, Pettigrew (1987) developed the Model of Strategic Change, which is based on the premise that strategic change cannot be regarded solely as a rational process undertaken by analysing the environments, suggesting alternatives and planning. Rather it is a complex, iterative process that is:

> shaped by the interests and commitments of individuals and groups, the forces of bureaucratic momentum, gross changes in the environment, and the manipulation of the structural context around decisions.
> (Pettigrew, 1987: p. 658)

The Model of Strategic Change identifies three dimensions of change: context, content and process. The *context* of change refers to those environmental factors that have influenced, restrained or provided the opportunity for change within the organisation. Referred to as the 'why' of change, consideration of the context within which the organisation is operating is important as it is the knowledge of these contextual factors and their interactions that provides the basis for understanding why change

Table 9.1 Contextual influences on public sport and leisure providers

External environment	Central policy initiatives to:
	    make local government transparent
	    increase accountability
	    continuously improve
	    challenge the role of the public sector
	Increases in health and safety legislation
	Changes to employment law
	Change in central government
	Increasing consumerism
	Ageing of the population
	Decreases in labour pool
	Rich/poor divide
	Social exclusion
	Decreases in budgets
	Changes in funding:
	    lottery
	    European Union
	Recession
	Increases in competition for customers
	Increasing influence of the 3 Es (efficiency, economy and effectiveness)
	Value for money
	Changes in data storage, transfer and retrieval
	Improvements in leisure technology

Internal environment	New managerialism Increasing professionalism Commercial practices Pressure to generate revenue Service re-organisation Decreases in staff numbers Impact of politicians

occurs. Although each environmental factor is important in its own right they do not act in isolation, but react and interact with each other and on occasion cancel each other out. A review of the operating contexts highlights the features outlined in Table 9.1 as leading to change in the management of public sport and leisure services.

The *content* of change refers to the particular change being considered. For example, this may be the introduction of quality programmes or performance management techniques. Being clear about 'what is different' allows an understanding of how and why the change has come about.

The third part of the Model for Strategic Change is the *process* by which change comes about. In their critique of the Model of Strategic Change, Spurgeon and Barwell (1991: p. 49) discussed how the model suggests that change within organisations often originates with a small subset of people who:

have become aware of a mismatch between the demands of a changing environment and the current performance of the organisation. If change is to be successfully implemented then this new perception of shortfall needs to gain legitimacy.

The process by which this occurs has been described by Pettigrew (1987: p. 658) as the 'actions, reactions and interactions from various parties as they seek to move the firm from its present to its future state'.

Thus, the model developed by Pettigrew (1987) provides the opportunity to consider not only key environmental factors, but allows these to be placed in the context of the historical, political and individual influences on the organisation. This allows managers to not only develop a holistic understanding of why particular change occurs, but also highlights the relationships that have to be considered when change is being planned.

Factors affecting the introduction of change

Public sport and leisure managers spend a significant part of their time carrying out activities that are intended to bring about change. As can be seen from Table 9.1, the environment within which they work is constantly changing and there have been a number of responses to this. In the past two decades, managers are likely to have:

- introduced new management techniques, such as quality management and performance management;
- changed service objectives in order to bring these in line with changes in central or local government;
- continually introduced new working practices or refined existing practices to take account of changes in health and safety legislation;
- offered jazzercise, then aerobic classes, followed by Boxercise, Step, Body Pump, Spin and Pilates, in order to meet changing customer tastes;
- hired and fired a number of staff;
- responded to changes in working time directives and the minimum wage;
- introduced new management information systems or equipment;
- overseen the refurbishment or re-decoration of facilities or equipment;
- had at least one change of title for the same job;
- changed jobs or responsibilities at least twice.

These changes have usually been introduced alongside the day-to-day running of their service. Therefore in order to be effective, public sport and leisure managers need to be able to identify the need for change and plan and manage the introduction of change, as well as carrying out their other duties.

There are a variety of factors that need to be taken into account in the management of change. The factors outlined below are the keys to ensuring that organisational change is implemented in an efficient and effective manner. Proactive managers will take account of these in the daily management of the organisation and will therefore be in a better position to respond rapidly to the changing environment if required to do so.

Adopting a contextual approach to change

As outlined above, an understanding of why change occurs and how change can be implemented requires managers to adopt a contextual approach to change (Pettigrew, 1987). This requires managers to be aware of the interactions of the environment within which they work, the process by which change can come about and the required change to be implemented. By being aware of the relationships between these three components, managers will be able to identify both the change that is required and change that will be accepted by the organisation (Pettigrew, 1987). This second point is paramount. In order for change to be accepted by the organisation it must be considered to be a legitimate response to the operating context and a legitimate response in terms of the organisational culture. If this is not the case, the change is unlikely to be effectively introduced into the organisation.

Environmental auditing

In order to identify potential areas of change, managers need to be aware of what is occurring in both their external and internal environments (Grant, 1995; Johnson and Scholes, 1999). They do this by a process of environmental auditing or 'scanning' of their operating environments in order to generate information about the environments and to identify trends that may suggest a need for change.

The process of environmental auditing is relatively straightforward. First, managers need to develop a structured approach to the collection of information, such as the use of the STEPV framework or internal audits outlined in Chapter 4. Second, managers need to analyse the information they have collected to identify factors that may require changes in operations or services. They then need to prioritise these areas in order to meet their service objectives. Finally, managers need to evaluate the impact of these changes on the operation of their service. Some changes may require an immediate response, while others may be changes required in the future that can be planned and implemented over time. In addition, the size of the change required needs to be evaluated, as does where it should occur within the organisation.

The purpose of environmental auditing is to assist managers to be proactive in the delivery of their public sport and leisure service. By being aware of the threats and opportunities in the external environment and the strengths and weakness of their internal environment, managers will be able to anticipate and plan changes required of their service. This means that managers must have a source of reliable information about both environments. Information about the internal environment will be gathered by talking to colleagues and staff and by being aware of what is occurring in the organisation. Information on the external environment may be harder to obtain, but is often provided by professional bodies, such as ILAM and ISRM and by networking with others who work in the industry.

An awareness of the organisation's culture

Chapter 3 discussed how managers need to understand the culture of the organisation in order to understand why decisions are made and how resources are allocated. An understanding of culture is even more important when considering the introduction of change into an organisation. As described in Chapter 3, the culture of the organisation reflects the beliefs and values that staff have about the organisation (Schein, 1985; Slack, 1997). Culture determines who will be powerful, what is important to the people in the organisation and the accepted ways of working. The introduction of change suggests that the accepted ways of working, or what is currently important are not good enough. As a result of this, staff will often resist change as they are comfortable with the existing priorities or ways of working. Therefore if managers want to introduce change, they need to be able to prevent or overcome this resistance by working with the existing culture. The reasons why staff resist change and how to overcome this will be discussed in detail below.

Knowledge of the culture of the organisation will help with the introduction of change in three ways. First, it will allow managers to identify facets of the organisation or its operations that cannot be changed without creating great resistance. For example, an organisation's logo may have historical or local significance or a particular shift pattern may have evolved to suit the most powerful members of staff and therefore attempts to change these will meet with strong resistance. Conversely, knowledge of the culture will highlight what can be changed and managers can use these aspects of the organisation to begin to introduce change to other aspects of the service. Third, an awareness of the culture will allow managers to determine who needs to be involved in the introduction of change in order to assist the process of implementation.

Good leadership

Leaders are those individuals who can influence other people on matters that are considered to be important (Gilgeous, 1997; Handy, 1993). In addition, leaders are those people who are expected to be and are seen to be influential on important matters. As a result, the successful introduction of change relies on the support of those who are considered to be leaders within an organisation. Without their support, change, particularly large-scale change, will be difficult to introduce. It is important to note that leaders are not necessarily managers. People with personal power or charisma (Chapter 3) will be seen by others in the organisation as influential and therefore managers need to be aware of who these individuals are. Often change fails to be introduced into public sport and leisure organisations because the people involved in promoting the change are not seen as influential.

Leaders have four roles to play in the introduction of change (Beer et al, 1990; Nadler, 1980). First, they need to generate a commitment to the change. This can be done by outlining why things need to be different and how the change will benefit the organisation. Second, they need to develop a shared vision of what the change will entail and how it will work in the future. It is much easier to generate support for change if everyone is clear about what and how things will be different. Third, leaders have a key role in implementing the change programme. They need to lead the activities that are required to bring about change and should be responsible for monitoring the process and help to overcome any resistance to the change. Finally, they have a responsibility to work in the manner required by the change. Leaders should be the first in the organisation to use new procedures or work to new objectives. This will allow the changes to be incorporated into the organisation's culture and to become the accepted way of working.

Use of power

The successful introduction of change requires the use of powerful people (Handy, 1993; Hersey *et al.*, 1996). As outlined above, the personal power associated with leadership allows leaders to generate commitment to and overcome resistance to change. In addition, managers may need the permission of those who have positional power to be able to implement change. There are also other sources of power that need to be considered in the effective introduction of change. Managers must ensure that they have adequate resources in order to develop and implement their intended changes. This means that the people who control the resources of the organisation must also support the change. Managers will also need to be aware of staff expressing negative power by resisting the proposed change.

Resistance to change

As was suggested above, most organisational change will lead to resistance among some or all staff. This is because the need to change implies that the current way of working is no longer adequate or acceptable and often staff will take this personally. It is also possible to argue that resistance to change is a logical reaction as individuals and indeed organisations function best in circumstances of stability. Nonetheless, resistance to change needs to be broken down if the change is to be fully integrated into the organisation.

Kanter (1989) identified that individuals have a variety of reasons for resisting change and managers need to be aware of which of the following is causing staff to resist change. If this is known, managers can then develop a strategy for overcoming this resistance. These are some of the possibilities:

- the 'difference effect': staff may resist change because they are concerned about what will be different in their working environment. They may be unclear about, or dislike, what the change means for their position, their workload or their working practices;
- concerns about competence: staff may be concerned about not being able to carry out the new tasks required of them or be unconvinced of their ability to use new equipment or technology. Therefore they will resist the introduction of a change that makes them feel or appear incompetent;
- loss of face: this is closely associated with the above two reasons for resisting change. If staff perceive that the change will lead to a loss of power or status in the organisation, or that they will look foolish or stupid, they will resist change;
- the 'ripple effect': resistance to change may not just come from those directly affected by the change. The introduction of change in an organisation usually has a ripple effect in that if change is introduced into one team or department, changes are usually required in other areas. For example, if facility managers implement a new booking system for customers, sports development workers will also have to use the new system. This may create confusion until the system is understood;
- more work: most changes require more work. Staff have to learn new procedures or ways of delivering services and this inevitably requires more work. They will often be required to attend training courses if new technology or new objectives are to be introduced. While this is essential, staff are usually expected to complete their usual workload, as well as attending the training sessions. This increase in workload will lead to resistance to the change;
- past resentments: the introduction of change may provide staff with the opportunity to express resentment about what has happened to them in the past. By exerting negative power, staff can hold up or prevent the introduction of proposed changes. For example, if a staff member thinks that they have missed out on a promotion, they may take the opportunity to express their resentment by undermining the need for change among their colleagues;

- real threats: in some instances change represents a real threat to staff, such as when redundancies need to be made. In this instance, resistance to change is understandable and is likely to be significant.

In addition to individual reasons for resisting change, staff as a whole, may exhibit a general desire not to change. This is because of:

- distorted perceptions: staff within the organisation either do not perceive that there is a threat in the external environment that requires them to change, or they perceive the threat but do not think that it is relevant to them and their service;
- dulled motivation: in this case staff perceive the threat but are not motivated enough to change in order to respond to the threat;
- failed creative response: dulled motivation often comes about because change that has been implemented in the past has failed or has been unsuccessful. A failed response to change makes organisational resistance to future change more likely;
- political deadlocks: the introduction of change must be acceptable to power groups within the organisation and occasionally change will be resisted because these groups cannot agree on what is needed. This leads to a deadlock that prevents change from being effectively introduced.

(Beer *et al.*, 1990)

Resistance to change is inevitable and managers need to have a strategy for dealing with it. Kotter and Schlesinger (1979) have suggested six strategies for dealing with resistance, which are dependant on the reason and the amount of resistance expressed. In many cases, more than one of the following strategies will need to be pursued, particularly if large-scale change in being introduced:

- education and communication: this strategy is proactive in that it aims to educate staff about the need for change prior to resistance being established. Information about the need for change, the process to be followed and the consequences of both changing and not changing allows staff to see the logic of the proposed change. This is a useful strategy for overcoming concerns about competence and the difference effect. In addition, it will break down existing distorted perceptions of the threat. This process can be carried out by one-to-one discussions, team meetings, by making presentations or via memos and reports;
- participation and involvement: this is the most effective strategy in overcoming all types of resistance to change. Involving staff in determining what change should be introduced and how this should be carried out will build commitment to the change as it is difficult for

staff to resist changes that they have been responsible for developing. Involvement can be at any stage, however, the more staff are involved at the initial stages, the more committed they will be. Staff can be involved in idea generation, allocated tasks that facilitate the introduction of change or asked to work with those who are resistant to the change. It is important, however, to ensure that staff have a meaningful and useful role to play in developing the change, otherwise resistance will become even greater;

- facilitation and support: this requires managers to work with their team members to overcome any concerns about what will be different and their competence. This is usually done on a one-to-one basis as the reasons for resisting change will be specific to individuals. This strategy is resource-intensive as it requires managerial time and specific skills in order to be successful. In addition the member of staff may still sometimes resist the change;

- negotiation and agreement: this requires managers to offer incentives to active and/or potential resistors and is often used to overcome political deadlocks or when individuals are resisting change due to past resentments or because of a real threat. It is an appropriate strategy when is it clear that some staff are going to be disadvantaged by the change. For example, when making people redundant, public sport and leisure services tend to offer better redundancy packages than what is legally required. This will appease unions and may encourage people to volunteer to be made redundant. This strategy is usually expensive and often is a short-term way of dealing with resistance as it does not deal with the underlying cause of the problem;

- manipulation and co-optation: these are covert attempts to influence those who are resisting change. Manipulation can occur by distorting the information that is given to those involved in the change, or by attempting to influence those who have power within the organisation by the selective use of information and restructuring of events. Co-optation involves overcoming resistance by incorporating those who are resisting change into the decision-making process. By placing these people into an important position in the change process, they are forced to work with the change, rather than against it. This is different from the strategy of involvement outlined above, in that individuals are given an important role in the process simply because they are resisting the change. These ways of overcoming resistance to change are bad for trust and often lead to others becoming resistant to the activities that have been carried out;

- coercion: this may be implicit or explicit and involves forcing staff to change. This may be done through threats of dismissal or loss of job status, and should only be used when it is imperative that the change is introduced and all other strategies for overcoming resistance have failed. Forcing individuals to change is problematic in that it builds up resentment, decreases the chances of the change being fully integrated into the organisation and breaks down the relationships between those being forced to change and those who are forcing the change.

Resistance to change is inevitable, however, it is important to note that not all resistance is a bad thing. Opposition to change may bring forward issues that managers had not considered which would have eventually had a negative impact on the proposed change. In most cases, resistance should be viewed as a means of identifying problems and managers then need to find ways of dealing with these problems. If resistance can be dealt with in an effective manner, staff commitment to the changes is likely to be stronger than if resistance did not occur.

Features of successful change

There are a number of features that increase the likelihood of change being implemented successfully. Although many of these seem obvious, once a potential solution has been identified it is easy for public sport and leisure managers to become overly concerned with the change they have identified and neglect issues to do with its successful introduction. The following features will not guarantee the successful implementation of change, but do they make it more likely.

A good idea

Although this seems obvious, the successful introduction of change is contingent on the change being perceived as being a good idea. It must be considered to be an appropriate response to changes in the operating environment and must fit within the culture of the organisation. If this is not the case, the proposed change will not be fully accepted into the working practices of the organisation. It is unlikely that all potential changes will be appropriate even if they appear to be a suitable response to changes in the operating context. Public sport and leisure managers must therefore involve others in deciding what changes should be introduced and seek feedback on any proposed change (Gilgeous, 1997; Senior, 1997). This will allow issues to be raised that had not necessarily been considered by the manager.

A knowledge of the factors that will promote or prevent change

Managers need to have a clear understanding of issues and factors within the organisation that will drive the process of change or act as a restraint. One of the main reasons that change fails in organisations is due to unexpected factors diverting attention and resources away from change or because the culture is not understood, nor resistance anticipated (Slack, 1997).

Lewin (1951) developed a technique known as *force field analysis* which allows the driving forces for change to be depicted against those resisting change. The theory underpinning force field analysis is that in any change situation there are forces for and against change. If these forces balance, then the organisation will not change. Therefore in order for change to be introduced, the forces for change have to be strengthened and/or the forces against change weakened. This will allow change to be introduced. The technique is relatively straightforward, consisting of four steps:

*   *Step 1*: the problem needs to be defined in terms of the present situation. This means stating clearly what the problem is, its strengths and weaknesses and the outcome to be achieved. For example, shift patterns need to change to allow the facility to be open earlier in the morning to meet customer requirements.
*   *Step 2*: the forces that will work for and against the proposed change need to be clearly identified. These can be based on people, resources, time, external factors and culture. It is important that these forces are generated through discussion with a number of people who have a vested interest in the change. If only the manager carries out this step, they are likely to miss issues that may not be of importance to them, but are of key importance to others.
*   *Step 3*: the forces then need to be rated in terms of their strength; i.e. high, medium or low. These should then be depicted in a force field diagram, using arrows of different lengths or widths to indicate the different strengths of the forces, as outlined in Figure 9.1. This allows their importance in the process to be determined and provides priorities for action.
*   *Step 4*: the most important forces need to be identified, which are usually those rated of high importance. For driving forces, a list of actions that will strengthen the force needs to be identified, followed by actions that will weaken the restraining forces. Those actions that will most help the introduction of change need to be incorporated into the change strategy, alongside the resources to make them happen.

Force field analysis is a powerful technique that can be used to convince staff and senior management of the need for change. It can provide a justification for action that is part of introducing change and allows resources to be prioritised. The force field diagram can also be used as a communication tool.

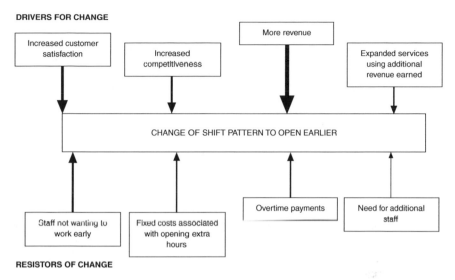

Figure 9.1 Force field analysis diagram for changing shift patterns.
Source: Adapted from Lewin, 1951.

An effective change team

This is particularly important for larger change or for a series of smaller changes that need co-ordination. In these cases it will be necessary to identify a team of people who will be responsible for promoting the changes required through commitment, communication and the provision of resources (Gilgeous, 1997; Pettigrew 1987; Senior 1997). An effective change team will be made up of a variety of individuals. First, it is important to ensure that all leaders are either part of the change team or are seen to support the team. Second, individuals who control necessary resources should also be part of the team. Third, it may be necessary to include individuals who represent the organisation's main political groups. Fourth, it is important that the team includes a spokesperson from the departments or staff groups that will primarily be affected by the proposed change. Finally, it is essential that senior management is seen to be supporting the change and should therefore be part of the team.

The size of the change team needs to be appropriate for the tasks that are required to be completed and in some cases, members of the team may change depending on the stage that the change is going through. In addition, members may have more than one role; for example, senior managers may also control the resources. It is important, however, that one or two individuals remain part of the team for the duration of the development and implementation of the change. These individuals can be considered to be the change 'champions' and have a responsibility to actively promote the introduction of the change.

Communicate the need for change

As outlined earlier, organisations and staff have a natural resistance to change as it challenges the organisation's culture and often means additional work. It is therefore essential that the need to change is communicated clearly and convincingly in order to break down resistance (Kotter and Schlesinger, 1979). This should be done in a consistent manner, ensuring that that no conflicting messages are issued. It is also important that all staff who are perceived to be promoting the change are communicating the same message.

One method of convincing staff of the need to change is to encourage dissatisfaction with the current state of the organisation. By highlighting weaknesses with existing practice and identifying how the organisation or staff will be disadvantaged by current practice is likely to encourage staff to be more open to the idea of change. It is important, however, that if this tactic is used that there is a clear vision of how the proposed change can overcome the weaknesses of the current system. This is the role of the change team and/or leaders in the organisation.

Employee commitment and involvement

Employee commitment to change is essential to ensure that the new way of working becomes integrated into the organisation's culture. The main way of gaining commitment to change is by involving staff in the development of potential changes and then in their subsequent introduction. Not only does this break down resistance to change, but it will also ensure that the implications of change and any potential difficulties are considered and understood by those who will be affected by the change.

Introduction of change at the appropriate level

Very few changes affect the entire organisation and when considering what needs to be different, it is important that public sport and leisure managers identify exactly what and who needs to change (Hersey *et al.*, 1996). This is to ensure that proposed change will bring about the desired outcome. For example, if certain members of staff are continually late for their shifts, their behaviour needs to change, rather than changing the shift pattern to encourage them to be on time. If a particular facility is performing poorly, it is important that changes are introduced into this facility, rather than the service as a whole.

There are three levels at which change can be introduced. First, there is the individual level where a member of staff may require new or additional training, or may require disciplining in order to amend their behaviour. Change at this level can be organised relatively quickly and is comparatively cheap. However, as change at this level is contingent on the individual changing, it is particularly important that they are aware of why they need to change and the benefits to them and the organisation of changing.

Second, change can be introduced at the group level and change at this level may affect a particular team or teams or a department. For example, a change in shift patterns will affect those who work on shifts, but not others who have more traditional working hours. A change in facility opening hours will affect all staff who work in that facility, but not staff who work at other facilities. Change at this level will require greater amounts of communication than change introduced at the individual level. It is also likely that greater amounts of resistance will be encountered and change at this level will usually require an implementation strategy. In addition, staff will need to be involved in the process.

Finally, change can be introduced at the organisational level, which may occur if organisational priorities are to change. CCT is an example of organisational change as it led to the restructuring of sport and leisure departments, a change of operating procedures for facilities and, in most cases, a change of organisational culture for those working in sport and leisure services. Introducing organisation change takes time; it will require the establishment of a change team and will need a structured implementation strategy as it is likely to be made up of a variety of smaller activities. Resistance will be encountered for a number of reasons and the introduction of the change will require negotiation and the acceptance of the organisation's culture and political systems. As a result, and due to the cost of such change, changes at the organisational level should only be attempted in rare circumstances. Such change may be appropriate if the organisation is facing a survival crisis (not often the case in public sport and leisure services) or if outside factors, such as legislation, require such a change.

Sufficient resources

The introduction of change needs to be supported by appropriate resources, such as money, staff training and staff time. Although money is important, allowing adequate staff time to develop and implement the change is even more so. One of the major factors that leads to the failure to effectively implement change is competition from alternative activities. Public sport and leisure managers are usually required to continue with their day-to-day duties on top of the activities that are required for the proposed change. In most situations managers will give their daily tasks priority as first, they understand how to do these and, second, these tasks need to be done so that the service can continue to function. This leads the activities associated with the change to be rated as a low priority. Managers need to be able to delegate some of their day-to-day work or ensure that other staff are also involved in developing and implementing change. They then need to make sure that these staff have adequate time to devote to the change activities.

An implementation strategy

The final feature in the successful introduction of change is a well-developed implementation strategy. This is particularly important when introducing large-scale change. All of the activities required to bring about the change need to be identified and put into an appropriate order. Tasks that are required must be allocated to those who will be responsible for these and the whole process needs to be communicated to all those who will be involved in and affected by the change.

Although the above features will assist with the successful introduction of change, managers also need to be aware of the factors that will cause difficulties with the introduction of change and these are outlined in Table 9.2. This factors need to be avoided and can be with careful planning and development.

Implementing change

Howell and Badmin (1996) and Kotter and Schlesinger (1979) have outlined and discussed a number of approaches to the way in which change can be introduced into public sport and leisure organisations. These are:

- the directive approach: this is the imposition of change on the organisation by management. It has little or no staff involvement and requires personal and positional power to be successful. This type of approach should only be used when a very small change is required or when all other approaches would fail. In addition, as it is a fast method of introducing change, a directive approach is appropriate when the survival of the organisation is under threat. Directive strategies may also be used when legislation makes change mandatory;
- the negotiating approach: this recognises that there are a number of groups that have to be involved in the change process. In this case, management would initiate the change process and would then enter into negotiations with key political groups. This approach is useful when compromise is required, or if one group is going to be disadvantaged by the proposed change. Negotiating approaches tend to develop compliance with the change, rather than commitment to it. Although this may allow the change to be introduced, it does not guarantee that the change will be fully accepted into the organisation and may lead to further negotiations in the future. A negotiating

Table 9.2 Difficulties in implementing change

Bad idea	If the proposed change is a bad idea it will not achieve the desired outcome and it will be difficult to generate commitment to the change. Change which is a bad idea can usually only be imposed by a directive approach and rarely becomes part of the organisation's culture.
Poor leadership and direction	Leaders have a responsibility to generate commitment to change and to develop a shared vision of how the change will benefit the organisation. If they are poor at doing this, or are not clear about the direction the organisation should be going, staff will not fully accept the proposed change.
Time taken	Change can be implemented too quickly and not allow staff to become committed to the change. This means that the new way of doing things is unlikely to become accepted practice, as staff will still value the old procedures. Alternatively, change can take too long to implement so that it either becomes inappropriate because of changing events or staff lose their motivation for the change.
Unidentified problems	If environmental auditing is not effective, or the change is not fully considered and planned, problems may arise with the proposed change that prevent it from being implemented. For example, building a major venue on a busy road will cause increased traffic congestion.
Uncontrollable environmental factors	These are factors that cannot be anticipated and that prevent change from occurring. This may be the resignation of a key member of staff or a significant decline in income due to factors such as the foot and mouth epidemic of 2000.
Inadequate co-ordination of activities	Change requires careful planning as it is usually made up of a series of smaller activities that need to be co-ordinated properly. Poor co-ordination will lead to difficulties or may increase resistance to the change. For example, sending staff on a training course to use new technology months before the technology is introduced is a waste of resources as they will forget how to use it.
Lack of skills	Introducing change is a complex process, particularly group or organisational level change. Managers and staff will not only need to be able to carry out the new procedures, or use the new technology, but they will also need skills associated with introducing change. Project management skills, the ability to communicate and convince, delegation, time management and flexibility will all be required.

approach would be appropriate when trying to change facility programmes, where managers may need to negotiate with different
groups of users in order for the change to be made;

- the normative approach: this type of approach is required for large
change or when staff within the organisation must be committed to
the change. This approach seeks to get people committed to the
change and to get it fully implemented into the organisation. It
requires staff involvement and participation, a good programme of
communication and adequate resources. It is time-consuming, but will
bring about effective change and will assist the proposed change to
become part of the organisation's culture. This type of approach is
appropriate when trying to bring about cultural change; for example,
developing a customer focus amongst staff or when organisational
objectives have changed;

- the analytical approach: this approach is appropriate when there is a
clear definition of the problem. It involves using experts or consultants
to develop a technically optimal solution. Although there may be some
consultation with staff, this is usually limited. This type of approach is
useful when the manager lacks the expertise to develop a solution to a
problem, or the organisation lacks the skills to be able to provide an
answer. It is not appropriate for change that requires the complete
commitment of staff, as the solutions proposed are unlikely to take
account of the culture or the organisation's politics – the solution will
be the most rational answer to the problem. An analytical approach is
appropriate for the development and implementation of management
information systems or specialised equipment;

- the action-centred approach: this is used when there is a general idea of
the problem, but no clear solution. Staff have the opportunity to
develop solutions and then try these out to see which is the most appropriate. This type of approach builds staff commitment to the change
and may allow staff to develop additional skills. It is time-consuming as
the most appropriate change may not be the first tried. In addition, it
may be costly as inappropriate change will lead to additional costs and
may lead to reductions in revenue if the service does not improve fast
enough to meet the needs of customers. An action-centred approach is
most appropriate when the change required is small-scale and does not
directly impact on the customer. An example of this may be a new
system for booking annual leave or a change in break times.

A manager's choice of approach will depend on several factors. First,
the pace of the change will affect the choice of approach. The faster the
change is required, the more directive an approach will need to be. If
change is long-term and can be introduced at a slower pace, then a normative approach may be more appropriate. It is worth noting that negotiating and action-centred approaches take time and therefore may not be

appropriate if the need for change is immediate. Second, the amount of resistance that is anticipated is important. If little resistance is anticipated, a directive or action-centred approach may be used. However, a directive approach may also be used when resistance is great, but change has to be introduced. Normative approaches are more effective at overcoming greater resistance and are useful when resistance arises because of a number of reasons. Third, the power base of the change leader will determine which approach is appropriate. If the person who is proposing the change is perceived to have a great amount of personal or positional power, then directive approaches are possible. Analytical approaches can be used when the initiator has expert power or when consultants will be used. Finally, the stakes involved are important. When the consequences of not changing are great, a directive or analytical approach becomes more appropriate. Conversely, when the consequences are not great, an action-centred approach may be appropriate as this allows staff to determine the change that is introduced.

Most change situations will require a number of these approaches. For example, there may be instances where an immediate response to a breach of health and safety rules is required and a manager will tell staff what has to be done. The development and introduction of the new operating procedures to prevent this breach from occurring again can be carried out via a normative, analytical or action-centred approach. What is important is that managers have a planned approach to the introduction of change. For example, if change is to be implemented via a normative approach, the associated levels of involvement, communication and education must be part of an implementation strategy. If an analytical approach is to be used, appropriate consultants or experts must be employed, information must be provided and then their recommendations need to be acted upon.

Summary and conclusions

The management of change is an ongoing and essential task for all public sport and leisure managers. The operating environments, particularly the external environment, will require managers to be continually refining the services they deliver. The key to the successful management of change is preparation and if managers are consistent and thorough in their environmental auditing, they will be proactive and effective in the management of change.

An understanding of people is also key to this process. Managers need to have the political skills to work within the culture and with the powerful groups within the organisation. They must know their staff well, so that they will be aware of where and why resistance may arise and how to deal with it. Most importantly, knowledge of the people involved in change will highlight who has to be involved in the process, what can be changed in the organisation and the most successful way to go about it.

Suggested tasks for further study

- Using the STEPV that was completed in Chapter 3, identify two factors in the external environment that will require public sport and leisure managers to make changes to their services.
- Suggest possible changes that can be made in response to these factors.
- Consider the best solution and identify why staff may be resistant to this change.
- What type of approach should be used to implement this change and why?

Further reading

Senior, B. (1997) *Organisational Change*, Harlow: Prentice Hall.

Part III
Public sport and leisure management

10 Best practice in public sport and leisure management

Game Plan: A strategy for delivering government's sport and physical activity objectives (DCMS/Strategy Unit, 2002: p. 183) has highlighted the critical role of local authorities in the delivery of the government's objectives for sport, stating that 'if participation is to be increased, it is at the local (not central or regional) level that most activity must be focused.' The importance placed on local authorities by central government underlines the need for good practice in the management of sport and leisure services. By implementing the best practices in the management areas of finance, human resources, performance and quality, managers will be in a better position to meet the demands of central government.

The Audit Commission (2002) has concluded that while sport and leisure services are performing well in comparison with other services, there are still some local authorities that need to make a fundamental change in their attitude towards the management of their sport and leisure services. The Commission highlighted the need for clearer objectives, better strategic planning, wider consideration of the options for delivery and a series of practical steps to improve services. Thus it would appear that, although most sport and leisure services are being run in a competent, skilled and professional manner, there are still a few that have yet to incorporate the management techniques outlined in this book.

The delay in adopting the approach to management outlined in this book must have detrimental consequences for the efficiency and effectiveness of the services within these local authorities. There is an abundance of evidence of the value of these practices to public sport and leisure services. Examples of best practice from Brighton and Hove, Belper, King's Lynn and West Norfolk, Sheffield and Taunton Deane Councils have been presented in this book. The DCMS/Strategy Unit (2002) report identifies the quality of Nottingham, Knowsley, Gateshead and Sunderland, while the Audit Commission (2002) also praises Sunderland, King's Lynn and West Norfolk. It is clear that these local authorities have in place many of the practices that make them exemplars in the delivery of the government's objectives for sport and recreation.

Consideration of the way these services are managed shows that these service providers have taken the management tools traditionally associated with the commercial sector and applied them to the public sector context. The adaptations required have been highlighted and discussed in the previous section of the book and it is clear that these tools are of significant value in the running of public sport and leisure services. Many of the adaptations that need to be made to meet the needs of the public sector context are minor. However, two features of the public sector require larger and more complex changes. The first of these is the need to meet social objectives, while the second is the greater accountability required of the public sector that is required of other sport and leisure providers.

Strategic planning is more complicated in the public sector due to the requirements of Best Value. First, local authorities have a legal requirement to consult with stakeholders, which although increasing accountability, is resource-intensive and time-consuming. Other sport and leisure providers can choose how, when and how much consultation they carry out. Second, public providers are required to evaluate other methods of delivering the service, or prove that they are the most competitive provider to the community. It is difficult to imagine a commercial sector organisation identifying the need to give their business up to a competitor.

The management of human resources is one area where the practices of the public, commercial, voluntary and charitable sectors are similar. This is primarily because HRM is heavily guided by legislation that impacts on all providers in the same way. A notable exception to this is in the area of equal opportunities, where the public sector tends to go beyond the legal minimum requirements for employment law and equal opportunities.

The financial management practices of the public sector have arguably changed the most over the past two decades, as they move towards the methods practised by the commercial sector. The diversity of funding sources that impact on local government makes the financial management of public sport and leisure services more complex than that of the commercial sector. However, public managers need to be able to read and understand financial accounts and use financial techniques for decision-making purposes.

The performance management framework outlined in Chapters 2, 4 and 7 is the lynchpin of the Best Value and CPA legislation and is a statutory requirement for the management of sport and leisure services. It is apparent from the Audit Commission (2000, 2002) that this framework, imported from the commercial sector, has much to offer public services. However, significant adaptations to this framework need to be made before it is completely appropriate for the public sector context.

First, the framework needs to be able to take account of social objectives. This means that managers will have to spend time in ensuring that these objectives are expressed clearly and that they have appropriate PIs. Without these two things, the framework will be meaningless. Second, any performance management frameworks used by the public sector need to be flexible enough to take account of changes in political priorities at both national and local level.

There is clear evidence of the value of quality management in the delivery of public sport and leisure services. This value is recognised by central government who have promoted the use of the Business Excellence Model in delivering Best Value. Of significant concern, however, is the capacity of quality management to take account of the social objectives of these services and Chapter 8 argued that the wholesale embracing of the ethos of quality may undermine the rationale for the delivery of public sport and leisure services. It is important that this weakness is taken into account when implementing quality management strategies. In addition, the use of a comprehensive and appropriate performance management framework will help to address this weakness as it should ensure that social objectives are set and met.

Finally, the management of change within public sector sport and leisure services needs to take account of the political nature of public services. Many of the activities associated with introducing change in the public sector are similar to those of the commercial, voluntary and charitable sectors. However, managers need to be aware of the expectations of politicians and central government. As political priorities can change suddenly and make change mandatory, the need for managers to be continually auditing their environments in order to prepare for change is essential.

Challenges for the future

Managers of public sport and leisure services spend much of their time identifying and responding to change occurring in their external environment. Indeed, this is one of the reasons why these services are now managed in a manner that reflects the practices of the commercial sector – a sector that has traditionally been considered to be more innovative and professional. From the discussions in this book, it is clear that public sector and commercial sector sport and leisure management have converged to such an extent that any difference is non-existent in many local authorities.

However, this does not mean that public sport and leisure managers can now become complacent, as the external environment continues to throw up issues that require a response. Three of the issues that public sport and leisure managers will need to deal with in the next few years are outlined below and responses to these will require innovative and strategic thinking, careful management of staff and resources and a commitment to customers and quality.

Improvements in information technology

A significant number of local authorities are already using information technology (IT) in the management and delivery of their services.

However, given the speed with which IT is advancing and an increasingly IT-literate general population, all sport and leisure services will have to integrate IT into their service delivery. This will need to be more than simply using IT for management information purposes. Customers will expect to be able to obtain information about services and make on-line bookings. In time they will expect to be able to view facilities and services via the web, eventually being able to have a 'virtual' sport and leisure experience.

This presents challenges for managers. First, customers will be highly critical of dated and slow IT. Managers will need to balance the cost of updating their technology with the costs of customer dissatisfaction. Second, as IT improves it will become a much bigger competitor for customers. As the 'virtual' technology improves, potential customers may be tempted to take their sport and leisure opportunities in their own houses, via technology. The technology will certainly offer a much wider range of activities than will be possible in public sport and leisure services.

Increasing customer expectations of services

Customer expectations of public sport and leisure services have increased steadily for the past two decades. Driven by the ease of travel and increasing competition, expectations of service quality are now at a point where it is becoming extremely difficult for managers of public services to meet them. This is because expectations are either so unrealistic that it is not possible to deliver services of such a high standard, or it is financially very costly to do so. This is particularly a problem for the public sector, given the levels of resource constraint. One of the main problems with expectations is that if managers meet customers' expectations so that they can compete in the market, customers then raise their expectations after a period of time. Managers are then trapped in a 'vicious cycle' of expectations where levels of service quality are expected to increase constantly.

It is difficult to see a solution to this, however, it may be possible for providers to 'manage' expectations by explaining to customers how their expectations are impacting on the service and providing information on why all expectations cannot be met. Although this may not solve the problem, it will reduce customer dissatisfaction as customers become aware of why their expectations are not being met.

Mixed funding sources

Although public sport and leisure services are still funded primarily through a grant from central government, managers often seek funding from other sources. This is primarily due to cuts in the grant from central government, but also because there is currently a wide variety of sources of funds for the public sector to utilize. Funding from European grants, lottery funding, Sport England and revenue-paying customers makes the financing of public sector services a complex issue. This will be exacerbated in future as more services establish charitable trusts and seek partnership with commercial providers, either as service deliverers or as part of a public/private partnership (PPP).

It is likely that the central grant to local authorities will continue to decline and lottery funding is certainly in decline. It will also get harder to obtain high levels of revenue from customers as competition in the industry continues to increase. However, PPP funding will become increasingly important and the government's objectives for sport and recreation may increase Sport England funding to local authorities. As a result, one of the financial management skills of the future will be the ability to identify when funding sources are declining and where to seek new funding. It will not be enough simply to understand how funding works and how to read financial accounts.

Summary and conclusions

The management of public sport and leisure services cannot operate in a vacuum and managers need to take into account and respond to developments in the external environment. This in turn requires managers to be aware of what is happening around them and to respond to these developments positively and logically, using the best practice discussed in this book. The potential contribution of sport and leisure to externalities such as improved health, crime reduction, opportunities for lifelong learning and better social cohesion, requires managers to demonstrate efficiency and effectiveness in the allocation of resources, management of staff and quality of service delivery. Failure to do this will lead to sport and leisure services being marginalised, or even shut down by the Audit Commission. Alternatively, if public sport and leisure managers do deliver services of Best Value, then continuity of funding and opportunities for enhanced resources should be forthcoming.

Bibliography

ACCA (2001) *Performance Management (study text)*, London: BPP Publishing.

Argenti, J. (1980) *Practical Corporate Planning*, London: Allen and Unwin.

Armstrong, H. (1997) 'Principles of best value', *News Release*, London: HMSO.

Audit Commission (1988) *Performance Review in Local Government: Data supplement*, London: HMSO.

Audit Commission (1989) *Sport for Whom?*, London: HMSO.

Audit Commission (1993) *Realising the Benefits of Competition*, London: HMSO.

Audit Commission (2000) *Aiming to Improve: The principles of performance measurement*, London: Audit Commission.

Audit Commission (2001) *Changing Gear: Best value annual statement 2001*, London: Audit Commission.

Audit Commission (2002) *Sport and Recreation: Learning from audit, inspection and research*, London: Audit Commission.

Barker, B.E. and Wilkinson-Riddle, G.J. (1998) *Balance Sheet Analysis for the IBM and Compatibles*, London: Pitman Publishing.

Batsleer, J. (1994) *Block One: People*, Foundations of Senior Management series, Milton Keynes: Open University.

Beardwell, I. and Holden, L. (2001) *Human Resource Management: A contemporary approach*, 2nd edn, Harlow: Pearson Education Limited.

Beer, M., Einstat, R.A. and Spector, B. (1990) 'Why change programs don't produce change', *Harvard Business Review*, November/December, pp. 158–166.

Beer, M., Spector, B., Lawrence, P., Quinn Mills, D. and Walton, R. (1984) *Managing Human Assets*, New York: The Free Press.

Bouwen, R. and Salipante, P.F. (1990) 'Behavioural analysis of grievances: episodes, actions and outcomes', *Employee Relations*, 12, 3, pp. 27–32.

British Standards Institute (1987) *Quality Vocabulary: Part 1, International Terms: BS 44778*, London: British Standards Institute.

Burns, T. and Stalker, G.M. (1961) *The Management of Innovation*, London: Tavistock.

Chartered Institute of Management Accountants (CIMA) (1996) *Management Accounting: Official terminology*, London: CIMA.

Clarke, F. (1992) 'Quality and service in the public sector', *Public Finance and Accountancy*, 23rd October, pp. 24–26.

Clarke, M. and Stewart, J. (1987) 'The public service orientation', *Local Government Policy Making*, Vol. 13, No. 4, March, pp. 34–40.

Coalter, F. (1990) in Henry, I. (ed.) (1990) *Management and Planning in the Leisure Industries*, Basingstoke: Macmillan Education.

Coalter, F. (1998) 'Leisure studies, leisure policy and social citizenship: the failure of welfare or the limits of welfare?', *Leisure Studies*, 17, pp. 21–36.

Coalter, F., Long, J. and Duffield, B. (1986) *Rationale for Public Sector Investment in Leisure*, London: Sports Council.

Collins, M. (2003) 'The trusts experience – do it for the services, not the money!', *Recreation*, June, pp. 24–27.

Cook, M. (1998) *Personnel Selection: Adding value through people*, 3rd edn, Chichester: Wiley.

Critten, P. (1994) *Human Resource Management in the Leisure Industry*, Harlow: Longman.

Davies, M. and Girdler, D. (2000) *Best Value: The pilot experience*, Essex: Centre for Amenity and Contracting Studies and Research.

DCMS (1999) *Policy Action Team 10: Report to the social exclusion unit – arts and sport*, London: HMSO.

DCMS/Strategy Unit (2002) *Game Plan: A strategy for delivering the Government's sport and physical activity objectives*, London: Strategy Unit.

Deming, W.E. (1986) *Out of the Crisis*, Cambridge: Cambridge University Press.

DETR (1998a) *Modernising Local Government: Improving local services through Best Value*, White Paper, London: Stationery Office.

DETR (1998b) *Modern Local Government: In touch with the people*, White Paper, London: Stationery Office.

Elcock, H. (1996) 'Local government' in Farnham, D. and Horton, S. (eds) (1996) *Managing the New Public Services*, 2nd edn, London: Macmillan.

Fayol, H. (1967) *General and Industrial Management* (Transl. Constance Storss), London: Pitman.

Fiedler, F. (1967) *A Theory of Leadership Effectiveness*, New York: McGraw-Hill.

Follett, M.P. (1924) *Creative Experience*, London: Longman.

Gaster, L. (1995) *Quality in Public Services*, Buckingham: OU Press.

Gilgeous, V. (1997) *Operations and the Management of Change*, Harlow: Prentice Hall.

Grant, R.M. (1995) *Contemporary Strategy Analysis: Concepts, techniques and applications*, 2nd edn, Oxford: Blackwell Business.

Gratton, C. and Taylor, P. (2000) *The Economics of Sport and Recreation*, London: E&FN Spon.

Guest, C. and Taylor, P. (1999) 'Customer oriented public leisure services in the United Kingdom', *Managing Leisure: An International Journal*, Vol. 4, No. 2, pp. 94–106.

Handy, C. (1993) *Understanding Organisations*, 4th edn, Harmondsworth: Penguin.

Hanson, A., Minten, S. and Taylor, P. (1998) *Graduate Recruitment and Development in the Sport and Recreation Industry: Final Report*, Sheffield: DFEE.

Henry, I. (2001) *The Politics of Leisure Policy*, 2nd edn, Basingstoke: Palgrave.

Hersey, P., Blanchard, K. and Johnson, D. (1996) *Management of Organisational Behaviour: Utilizing human resources*, 7th edn, USA: Prentice Hall.

HMSO (1991) *The Citizen's Charter*, London: HMSO.

Holloway, J. (1999) 'Managing performance', in Rose, A. and Lawton, A. (1999) *Public Services Management*, Harlow: Pearson Education Limited.

Honey, P. and Mumford, A. (1992) *The Manual of Learning Styles*, Maidenhead: Honey.

Horton, S. and Farnham, D. (1999) *Public Management in Britain*, London: Macmillan Press Ltd.

Houlihan, B. (1991) *The Government and Politics of Sport*, London: Routledge.

Houlihan, B. (2001) 'Citizenship, civil society and the sport and recreation professions', *Managing Leisure: An International Journal*, Vol. 6, No. 1, pp. 1–14.

Howat, G., Crilley, G., Absher, J. and Milne, I. (1996) 'Measuring customer service quality in sports and leisure centres', *Managing Leisure: An International Journal*, Vol. 1, No. 2, pp. 77–90.

Howell, S. and Badmin, P. (1996) *Performance, Monitoring and Evaluation in Leisure Management*, Great Britain: Pitman.

Johnson, G. and Scholes, K. (1999) *Exploring Corporate Strategy*, Europe: Prentice Hall.

Jones, G., George, J. and Hill, C. (1998) *Contemporary Management*, USA: McGraw-Hill.

Juran, J.M. (1988) *Juran on Planning for Quality*, London: Collier Macmillan.

Kanter, R.M. (1989) *When Giants Learn to Dance*, USA: Simon and Schuster.

Kaplan, R. and Norton, D. (1996) *The Balanced Scorecard*, Boston: Harvard Business Press.

Katz, D. and Kahn, R.L. (1966) *The Social Psychology of Organisations*, New York: Wiley.

Kotter, J.P. and Schlesinger, L.A. (1979) 'Choosing strategies for change', *Harvard Business Review*, 57, pp. 106–124.

Lawrence, P. and Lorsh, J.R. (1967) *Organisation and Environment*, Boston: Harvard University.

Lawton, A. and Rose, A. (1994) *Organisation and Management in the Public Sector*, London: Pitman.

Leisure Futures (1994) 'Has CCT led to better quality services?', Reading: ILAM.

Lentell, R. (2000) 'Untangling the tangibles: physical evidence and customer satisfaction on local authority leisure centres', *Managing Leisure: An International Journal*, Vol. 5, No. 1, pp. 1–16.

Lewin, K. (1951) *Field Theory in Social Science*, New York: Harper and Row.

Local Government Training Board (1987) *Getting Closer to the Public*, Luton: LGTB.

Luker, R. (2000) 'US sports sector slips from the summit', *SportBusiness*, March, pp. 48–49.

McDonald, M. (1999) *Marketing Plans: How to prepare them, how to use them*, Oxford: Butterworth–Heinemann.

March, J.G. and Simon, H.A. (1958) *Organisations*, New York: Wiley.

Mayo, E. (1933) *The Human Problems of Industrial Civilisation*, New York: Macmillan.

Meyer, A. and Blümelhuber, C. (1998) 'Quality: not just a trend, but a strategic necessity in professional sports', *European Journal for Sport Management*, September, pp. 55–81.

Mintel (2000) *Family Leisure Trends*, Market Report, London: Mintel International Group.

Mintzberg, H. (1979) *The Nature of Managerial Work*, Englewood Cliffs: Prentice-Hall.

Mullins, L.J. (1996) *Management and Organisational Behaviour*, London: Pitman.

Murphy, W. (1986) 'Professionalism and recreation provision in local government and industry', in Coalter, F. (ed.) (1986) *Leisure, Politics, Planning and People – Vol. 24 The politics of leisure*, Eastbourne: Leisure Studies Association.

Nadler, D.A. (1980) 'Concepts for the management of organisational change', in Tushman, M. and Moore, W. (1988) *Readings in the Management of Innovation*, London: Ballinger Publishing.

Nichols, G. (1996) 'The impact of compulsory competitive tendering on planning in leisure departments', *Managing Leisure: An International Journal*, Vol. 1, No. 2, pp. 105–115.

Nichols, G. and Robinson, L. (2000) *The Process of Best Value – Further lessons from the leisure pilots*, Melton Mowbray: Institute of Sport and Recreation Management.

Nichols, G. and Taylor, P. (1993) 'A case study of a partnership between the public and voluntary sector to reduce crime', *Local Government Policy Making*, Vol. 23, No. 3, pp. 30–36.

Nichols, G. and Taylor, P. (1995) 'The impact on local authority leisure provision of Compulsory Competitive Tendering, financial cuts and changing attitudes', *Local Government Studies*, Vol. 2, No. 4, pp. 607–622.

Office of the Deputy Prime Minister (2001) *Implementing Best Value – A consultation paper on draft guidance*, London: ODPM.

Office of the Deputy Prime Minister (2002) *Strong Local Leadership – Quality Public Services*, London: ODPM.

Parasuraman, A., Zeithaml, V. and Berry, L. (1988) 'A multi-item scale for measuring customers perceptions' of service quality', *Journal of Retailing*, 64, 8, pp. 12–40.

Parasuraman, A., Zeithaml, V. and Berry, L. (1994) 'Alternative scales for measuring service quality: a comparative assessment based on psychometric and diagnostic criteria', *Journal of Retailing*, 70, 3, pp. 201–230.

Patmore, D. and Tomes, A. (1994) 'Quality: the engine of cultural change', *Local Government Policy Making*, Vol. 21, No 2, October, pp. 3–7.

Pearce, C.G. (1993) 'How effective are we as listeners?', *Training and Development*, April, p. 15.

Pettigrew, A. (1987) 'Context and action in the transformation of the firm', *Journal of Management Studies*, Vol. 26, No. 4, 649–670.

Pettigrew, A., Ferlie, E. and McKee, L. (1992) 'Shaping strategic change', London: Sage.

Pfeffer, N. and Coote, A. (1991) *Is quality good for you? – A critical review of quality assurance in Welfare Services*, Social Policy Paper, No. 5, Institute for Public Policy Research.

Pollitt, C. (1993) *Managerialism and the Public Services*, 2nd edn, Oxford: Blackwell.

Poole, M. and Warner, M. (1998) *The IEBM Handbook of Human Resource Management*, London: Thomson Learning.

Quick, J.C. and Quick, J.D. (1984) *Organisational Stress and Preventative Management*, New York: McGraw-Hill.

Rees, W.D. and Porter, C. (2001) *Skills of Management*, 5th edn, London: Thomson Learning.

Robins, S.B. (1994) *Essentials of Organisational Behaviour*, 4th edn, New Jersey: Prentice Hall.

Robinson, L. (1997) 'Barriers to Total Quality Management in public leisure services', *Managing Leisure: An International Journal*, Vol. 2, No. 1, January, pp. 17–28.

Robinson, L. (1999a) *The Introduction of Quality Management to Local Authority Leisure Services*, Doctoral thesis: Loughborough University.

Robinson, L. (1999b) 'Following the quality strategy: the reasons for the use of quality management in UK public leisure facilities', *Managing Leisure: An International Journal*, Vol. 4, No. 4, pp. 201–217.

Robinson, L. (2002) 'Is quality management appropriate for public leisure services?', *Managing Leisure: An International Journal*, Vol. 7, No. 1, pp. 33–40.

Robinson, L. and Crowhurst, M. (2001) *Quality Programmes in Public Leisure Services*, Melton Mowbray: ISRM.

Robinson, L. and Wolsey, C. (1996) 'Considerations in developing the public service orientation', *Local Government Policy Making*, Vol. 23, No. 1, July, pp. 65–70.

Rogers, C. (1951) *Client-centred Therapy: Its current practice, implications and theory*, Boston: Houghton Mifflin.

Rose, A. and Lawton, A. (1999) *Public Services Management*, Harlow: Pearson Education Limited.

Russell, D., Patel, A. and Wilkinson-Riddle, G.J. (2002) *Cost Accounting: An essential guide*, London: Pearson Educational Ltd.

Sanderson, I. (1992) *Management of Quality in Local Government*, Longman: Harlow.

Sanderson, I. (1998) *Achieving Best Value through Performance Review*, Warwick/DETR Best Value series, Paper No. 5, Coventry: Warwick University.

Schein, E. (1985) *Organisational Culture and Leadership*, San Francisco: Jossey-Bass.

Senior, B. (1997) *Organisational Change*, Harlow: Prentice Hall.

Sims, A. and Smith, R. (2000) *Management Accounting Business Strategy*, London: CIMA.

Slack, T. (1997) *Understanding Sport Organisations*, Leeds: Human Kinetics.

Sloman, J. and Sutcliffe, M. (1998) *Economics for Business*, London: Prentice Hall.

Sport England (1999) *Best Value through Sport: The value of sport*, London: Sport England.

Spurgeon, P. and Barwell, F. (1991) *Implementing Change in the NHS*, London: Chapman and Hall.

Stabler, M. (1996) 'The emerging new worlds of leisure quality: does it matter and can it be measured?', in Collins, M. (ed.) *Leisure in Different Worlds, Vol. 2 Leisure in industrial and post-industrial societies*, pp. 249–268, Eastbourne: Leisure Studies Association.

Stabler, M. and Ravenscroft, N. (1994) 'The economic evaluation of output in public leisure services', *Leisure Studies*, 13, pp. 111–132.

Stevens, D. and Green, P. (2002) 'Explaining continuity and change in the transition from Compulsory Competitive Tendering to Best Value for sport and recreation management', *Managing Leisure: An International Journal*, Vol. 7, No. 2, pp. 124–138.

Taylor, F.W. (1972) *Scientific Management*, USA: Greenwood Press.

Taylor, P., Robinson, L.A., Bovaird, A., Gratton, C. and Kung, S. (2000) *Performance Measurement for Local Authority Sports Halls and Swimming Pools*, London: Sport England.

Thomas, K.W. (1976) 'Towards multi-dimensional values in teaching: the example of conflict behaviours', *Academy of Management Review*, Vol. 12, pp. 484–490.

Thomson, R. (1997) *Managing People*, 2nd ed., Oxford: Butterworth–Heinemann.

Torkildsen, G. (1999) *Leisure and Recreation Management*, 4th edn, London: E&FN Spon.

Walsh, K. (1991) 'Quality and public services', *Public Administration*, Vol. 69, Winter, pp. 503–514.

Watt, D. (1998) *Sports Management and Administration*, London: E&FN Spon.

Williams, C. and Buswell, J. (2003) *Service Quality in Leisure and Tourism*, Wallingford: CABI Publishing.

Wilson, D. and Game, C. (1994) *Local Government in the United Kingdom*, Basingstoke: Macmillan.

www.axiom-e.co.uk/index (2002) 'Defining financial terms', accessed September 2002.

Index

Business Link 145

Calderdale Council 27
capital, and financial accounting 106–7,
    111
catering services 4
CCT (Compulsory Competitive
    Tendering) 10–11, 34; as an example
    of organisational change 167; negative
    impacts of 30; and new managerialism
    29–31; and organisational culture 54;
    and performance management 132;
    and professionalisation 18; and public
    sport and leisure delivery mechanisms
    14
central government: and change
    management 177; control of local
    authorities 33–4; and the
    development of public sport and
    leisure services 7–10, *see also*
    legislation
certainty, decision-making under
    conditions of 42, 43
change management 153–72, 177;
    contextual approach to
    understanding 154–6; effective
    change teams 165–6; and
    environmental auditing 155, 157–8;
    factors affecting the introduction of
    change 155, 156–9; factors
    promoting or preventing 163–4;
    features of successful change 163–8;
    implementing change 168–71; and
    leadership 158–9; and organisational
    culture 158; and power 159;
    resistance to change 159–63, 171;
    and resources 167–8; structural
    approach to understanding 153–4
charitable trusts 179
Charter Mark 144, 146, 148–9
CIMA (Chartered Institute of
    Management Accountants) 99
Citizen's Charter 25
citizenship rights: and participation in
    sport and leisure 5; and subsidy of
    public facilities 150
Clarke, F. 136–7
classical approach to management 37
Coalter, F. 17, 18
coercion, overcoming resistance to
    change 162–3
collaborating, and conflict management
    46, 47

commercial sport and leisure services:
    and human resource management 97;
    objectives of 35; and performance
    management 133
commercial and voluntary sectors:
    competition from 7; and new
    managerialism 21
communication: and external
    (outreach) workers 96; managerial
    communication skills 44–5;
    overcoming resistance to change 161
community services 4, 151
community workers 5
comparison: and performance
    management 129–31; of sport and
    leisure performance 12, 73–4
competence concerns, and resistance to
    change 160
competing, in conflict management 45,
    47
competition, and the emergence of new
    managerialism 26–8
competitive strategy, and financial
    management 100–1
competitiveness, demonstrating 12,
    74–5
Comprehensive Performance
    Assessment *see* CPA (Comprehensive
    Performance Assessment)
compromising, in conflict management
    46, 47
Compulsory Competitive Tendering *see*
    CCT (Compulsory Competitive
    Tendering)
conflict management 45–8
conservation services 4
Conservative government (1980s and
    1990s) 9, 25; hostility to local
    authorities 28; and strategic planning
    63
consultation 12; and strategic planning
    72–3
consumerism 155; and new
    managerialism 23–6, 27
Consumers' Association 23–4
contingency approach to management
    38–9
continuing staff development 89–91;
    induction 89–90, 92; training 91–2
controllability, and performance
    management 132
Cook, M. 82
Coote, A. 23–4